Politically Incorrect

And Proud Of It

Copyright © 2021 by David L Roberts
All Rights Reserved.

Written and Edited by David L Roberts

Self-Published Through
Kindle Direct Publishing

A Very Different Disclaimer

There is no need for the typical disclaimer, because it would serve no purpose. These are my own thoughts, beliefs and opinions that I strongly believe. I don't seek to slander or malign any individual or group, but I will not hide or deny my own beliefs and feelings. I apologize for nothing and accept full responsibility for the content of this book and the views and comments contained herein. I am who I am, a sinner saved by the grace of GOD and a Republican card carrying conservative Christian.

David L Roberts

LIST OF TOPICS

INTRODUCTION

This book is a collection of personal thoughts, observations, memories and some interesting short stories on various subjects. Loosely arranged they cover a wide variety of topics and a number of years.

I'm not writing a bestseller, I'm just doing what a lot of people want to do, say or write what is on their mind and what they believe to be the truth about many different issues. I'm not politicly correct, and I never will be. Just because some liberal fool comes along and says that a word or term is suddenly offensive is not an adequate reason for me to change. Are there some words that should no longer be used, of course, but those were wrong right from the start.

My purpose in writing this book isn't to convince you to believe as I do, but to express what I believe to be the truth on issues we all face at some time. I know my opinions will not be shared by many groups, but one important thing you should know about me is I don't debate, argue or try to convince anyone to agree with me. You're entitled to your opinions and I don't care what they are or if you agree with mine. I'm just telling you why I'm right on these subjects and the reasons why I'm right.

Now here is a small collection of my very own, wise and profound, but mostly useless and forgettable thoughts and ideas. Oh, yah and some very blunt personal opinions too. Let's start off with a poem that I wrote and some light subjects and observations about people.   Then we'll get into the meat of my opinions about family, government, and some important social issues of the day.   Lastly, we'll go down memory lane just for fun and look at some of the great events of our past and a few short stores you might enjoy. So, get yourself a cup of coffee or whatever your favorite refreshment is, find a comfortable spot and let me tell you why I'm politically incorrect and proud of it.

"In My Lifetime"

In my lifetime, I've stood silently in the shadows of great mountain ranges and gazed upwards at their majestic beauty and grandeur.

I've flown high above the earth and as I looked down at the splendid beauty of GOD's creation I recalled Genesis 1:31 "And GOD saw everything that He had made, and behold, it was very good.

I've sailed across the vast oceans of the world and gazed upon sparkling blue waters as the last fleeting rays of sunlight faded below a distant horizon. At that moment I could find no words to describe the beauty my eyes were privileged to see.

I've witnessed the rich colors of a new rainbow after a raging ocean storm. As it stretched across the clearing sky to a distant horizon I thought, how powerful thou are and beautiful is your mercy Lord?

I've been humbled on a stary night over a calm ocean, and as I gazed upward at your vast universe I asked, out of all these endless stars that I see, who am I Lord, that you should know me.

Having seen all these beautiful creations by GOD's own hand, can my mind now dare to imagine, how glorious Heaven will be?

SECTION ONE
THINGS ABOUT PEOPLE THAT IRRITATE ME

In these first three sections, I've come up with a variety of subjects. Some things about people that irritate me, some things I don't understand and some serious events or subjects that really make me mad.

1. People that talk loud about themselves in a crowd or on a phone, obviously so everyone nearby will hear what they're saying and be impressed.

2. Someone that asks you a question, but they love the sound of their own voice so much they won't shut up long enough for you to answer.

3. The person that can't stop laughing at their own story or joke and they haven't even got to the punch line yet.

4. No matter what the subject the guy that has done it or has to "one up" your story, such as: if you raced on weekends he drove the pace car one time at Daytona. If you were in the Army then this guy was in special forces. No matter what you have done or where you've been this guy has already been there, done that, and got the trophy.

5. Your're on the freeway and a quarter of a mile from your exit when some guy speeds up and cuts in front of you even though he is getting off at the same exit.

6. You're on the freeway and you come up behind someone in the center lane. The person is under the speed limit so you've had enough and pull into the left lane and speed up. As you pass by you look over and see some teenager or maybe a "soccer mom" and their on their phone with no idea of what's going on. So many different words and phrases run silently through my mind.

7. People that interrupt when someone else is speaking or the person that continueously talks over someone when that other person is still talking.

8. When I'm at a fast food restaurant I may have them add or leave an item off my burger or substitute onion rings for fries. It really irritates me though when someone wants to stand there for five minutes inventing something that's not even on the menu. If you can't eat what they serve then go home and make it yourself.

9.   Those people that are habitually late. They can't seem to get to work on time. They're the ones that are always running into church 5 minutes after the music has started. How about the friends you've invited over for dinner at 7:00 PM and it's now 7:10 PM and the meal is already on the table. I swear there are people out there that somehow they will be late for their own funeral.

10. If you're in a public place such as a park use you earbuds to listen to your music the rest of us are there for some relaxing quite moments.   I don't care how loud you play your radio in your car just leave the windows UP.   Everyone else doesn't want to hear your music at an ear shattering 120 decibels, damage your hearing not mine.

11. People and their disruptive, out of control kids in public places like shopping malls. I just don't believe some parents that let their children run through stores grabing anything they want. How about the ones that are just crying and screeming to the top of their lungs and mom or dad are acting like they don't even hear them, the rest of us do! The parents just say, I can't control them; I don't know what to do; or how about it's none of your business. How about you take your kids out of the store get them under control or take them home and tan their little hides. The real problem is the lack of parenting.

SECTION TWO
THINGS ABOUT PEOPLE I DON'T UNDERSTAND

1. Fist bumping, now what is that all about? Two grown men greeting one another by bumping their fists against each other or their elbows. Is that some kind of masculine tribal ritual? What's wrong with a good ole firm handshake? People have become such germ-a-phobes and won't even take a man's hand in greeting. If you have a cold then tell the person, they'll understand. I guess I still believe in the old traditions. Look a man in the eye, shake his hand and always remove your hat when greeting a lady. [Update 1/26/21: COVID-19, no touching those outside your household until this virus is under control and always wear your mask when leaving home.]

2. I don't understand why some people allow their houses or mobile homes to look like shacks and their yards to look like the city dump. I know there are many folks that can't afford to fix up their homes, but there are some things that could be done so that they look like someone cares.

The yards are a different story though. I hate seeing places where there are all kinds of objects left in the yard rusting as the grass grows up around them. Bushes that have never been trimmed and 2 or 3 cars in the grass that obviously don't run any longer. People, a rusty old Ford, rotting tires or a broken toilet is not considered yard art, in most areas! Have some pride, clean it up!

3. I don't understand why the media, politicians and the American people care what Hollywood thinks about politics or the social issues that face us today?   It seems like no matter what the subject, every time something big hits the news, some reporter sticks a camera and a microphone in front of some Hollywood personality for a statement.

Who decided that an actor or Hollywood executive was an expert on political issues, religion, immigration, gun control or any other issue? They entertain us and we love that, but just because they have access to TV cameras and the media doesn't mean America wants to hear their personal opinions as if we're not smart enough to determine what the facts are on our own.

Also, why does everyone in the entertainment media and the tabloid newspapers think we need to know anything about the private lives of those in the performing arts. In my opinion those tabloids and celebrity magazines are mostly read by people with no life and too much time on their hands. I don't know anything about the private life of my doctor or dentist and the life and times of my insurance agent is not going to make the tabloids.

The performing arts is a profession just like everyone else's, so let them entertain us and keep their private life, private. After all they're "ACTORS," they live in a fantasy world, so why should anyone believe anything they say on any real-world subject?

4. When I walk into Wal-Mart why do I hear Christmas music and see Christmas decorations and it's only the first of September? Or how about commercials that say, "Christmas in July!" Talk about getting a jump on sales! Now day's stores are putting up all the holiday decorations and products at the same time. You walk down one isle and it's Halloween, the next it's Thanksgiving and of course all over the store it's Christmas. I remember a time when it wasn't Christmas until Santa Claus made his entrance at the end of the Macy's Thanksgiving Day Parade.

I believe we should celebrate the spirit of Christmas, Jesus Christ and the joy of eternal salvation year-round and not just save it for one day. However, I still refuse to sing "Jingle Bells" in October or put my Christmas tree and lights up before Thanksgiving. And to those of you that leave your outdoor Christmas lights up year-round because of physical limitations I understand. If your turning your outdoor lights on year-round, well I've been a neighborhood "yard of the month" judge before and take my word for it in most locations you're not going to win in July with them.

5. I don't understand why caskets cost thousands of dollars and why people are willing to pay between $3,000 to $10,000 or even more for a fancy box that you're going to take to the cemetery and bury it, never to been seen again. That makes absolutely no sense at all. The dearly departed could care less and a year later you're not going to remember what it was, only that you paid a lot of money for it. Cremation is the way to go, and the burial urn and internment only costs a couple of thousand dollars. Ashes to ashes, dust to dust.

6. I don't understand why people want tattoos. I spent 26 ½ years in the Navy and people will sometimes ask me what tattoos I have, and I will immediately answer something like this. "I've been in dozens of ports of call around the world; I've been to Washington D.C.; 35 of our 50 states; 4 of the 7 continents; 19 countries; sailed 5 of the 7 seas. I've crossed the Equator; the International Date Line; the Prime Meridian and the Mason Dixie Line and there's not a tattoo anywhere on this body." I won't go as far as to condemn anyone for having them, I know a lot of people do, but I just don't understand the attraction and the need to willingly deface what God created.

When I worked at DFW Airport I use to see girls as young as 14 years old and they would have tattoos on their necks and ankles. Sometimes when they bent over to put their shoes back on at the security checkpoint you would see one peeking out just above their rear waistband. Why would parents let a child do that? Then I would see their mother bent over right next to them with the same tattoo. Question answered!

7. At the time of this entry there is an old debate that has come back up again in some resent news stories. Why do we need the government to issue a marriage license? GOD has commanded that a man will leave his father and mother and be united with his wife and its GOD that has ordained the institution of marriage between one man and one woman.

The federal or state governments have no constitutional or Biblical responsibility of being in the business of marriage and there is absolutely no reason for any state to issue a marriage license. Their only excuse is to collect more taxes or fees to fund projects and programs we most likely don't need or to line someone's pockets. I say let the government ensure the fair and equal distribution of benefits to individuals and leave what GOD has created and ordained up to GOD.

8. This next subject is not something that I don't understand, it's just something that bothers me sometimes when I think about it. Death, it's something that we all think about from time to time and it's something we will all have to come to terms with at some point in our lives. As we get older, we begin too loose grandparents, few friends, and eventually our parents and even a spouse. During 2020 I lost 2 friends and at this very moment my sweet mother in law is in home hospice care and may pass away at any time.

As we reach our so called golden years, we seem to be attending more funerals than weddings depending on the number of children and grandchildren you have. So many of us tend to dwell on our own mortality and how much longer do we have before those around us will be attending our funeral. For some people, it becomes an obsession that can make them very bitter or very withdrawn to the point that their final years are sometimes very sad and lonely. Please don't be that person.

Some of us worry, have we properly set things in motion for our spouses and children so that they will be taken care of. What should we do before that day comes upon us? I'm guilty of doing all of this and I'm quickly finding out that the best thing to do is take care of everything you can, don't worry about what you have no control over and live life like there's no tomorrow, because there may not be. It's not the quantity of time, but the quality of time you spend with the people that are important to you. Make it all count, make memories with them, and for them.

Matt. 6:34 "Therefore do not worry about tomorrow, for tomorrow will worry about its own things. Sufficient for the day is its own trouble." [1]

9. I don't understand these hyphenated names that people like to use to identify themselves, like African-American, Jewish-American or Japanese-American, when they were born in Dallas, New York or Oxford, Mississippi. I may have a Welsh or German ancestry, but I was born in Fort Worth, Texas, so I'm a Texan. More importantly I'm an American and proud of it.

Now if someone is born in say, Tokyo and they immigrate (legally) to the United States and go through the process of becoming a U.S. citizen, then yes that's what I would call a Japanese-American. However I would hope that they would soon just call themselves a proud American.

I think it's stupid when you have these people that haven't set foot outside of their own city of birth or state and they want to connect their identity to some other nationality. They're no more African, Italian or Chilian than I'm an Eskimo and a lot of them couldn't find another continent on a map if their next breath depended on it.

If you're a citizen of this country then claim it, stop being divisive and be proud of your citizenship and your country. With all our faults, this country is still the freest, most blessed and most inclusive nation in the world. If you don't believe it, travel to some other countries, like Africa or the Middle East.

10. Black Lives Matter's (BLM) another "I'm a victim group" is trying to get as many headlines as they can these days. Their mission statement states in part, "Black Lives Matter Global Network Foundation, Inc. is a global organization in the US, UK, and Canada, whose mission is to eradicate white supremacy and build local power to intervene in violence inflicted on Black communities by the state and vigilantes." [2]

My version "Black Lives Matter, Global Network of thugs, thieves and terrorists whose objective it is to remove all other races from power and from the face of the earth. To establish black power in all communities in order to facilitate chaos and mass hysteria in the lives of all communities." The short of it is, they're just another terrorist group that wants a stage in order to blame someone else for their lot in life.

To me they're just wanting a free ride on the money and backs of others, and they don't want to take personal responsibility for their actions and their own lives. Government handouts, free programs, looting, theft and robbery are all acceptable ways of life to them.

I just don't understand, if they would put all that energy towards improving themselves, they might have fewer problems. Many of them could care less about the cause, their just paid trouble making thugs. In the Bible I study and the way I was brought up, **ALL Lives Matter**, from conception to the oldest one of us. I'm reminded of a quote by Ronald Reagan:

"We must reject the idea that every time a law's broken, society is guilty rather than the lawbreaker. It is time to restore the American precept that each individual is accountable for his actions." [3]

11. Entitlements, "A sense of entitlement is a personality trait that is based on a person's belief that they deserve privileges or recognition for things that they did not earn. In simple terms, people with a sense of entitlement believe that the world owes them something in exchange for nothing."[4]

Why do so many people believe they are entitled to something they didn't earn or deserve. They say the "Millennial Generation" is the entitlement generation, but is it, or is it the mind set of just about everyone in today's world society. I hate the TV commercial I hear with this actor saying, "I'm calling right now, because I want everything I'm entitled to." For the life of me these statements and people with this attitude just drive me crazy.

Just what are people entitled to? Our Declaration of Independence says, "We hold these truths to be self-evident, that all men are created equal, that they are endowed by their Creator with certain unalienable Rights, that among these are Life, Liberty and the pursuit of Happiness." But so many of them and their distorted interpretation of the founding documents believe they are entitled to just about everything needed for daily life and enjoyment. "I want what I want, you owe it to me, and I want it now," seems to be the slogan for so many in our country today.

Are people entitled to free food, free shelter, free medical health care, and are people even entitled to work. The majority of us need a hand up at some point in our lives, but handouts, "freebees" have to be temporary, not a way of life. My belief is, if you don't earn it, if you don't produce it, if you don't buy it, it's not yours and you don't deserve it.

12.   I don't understand why "We The People" keep re-electing the same crazy, inept, bungling politicians.   We gripe and complain about what they're doing from our cities to Washington D.C. and then come election time we vote the same individuals right back in office. Are we overwhelmed in this country by stupid people electing stupid people over and over again?   And the craziness is going on in both Democrat and Republican Parties, mostly Democrat. When are Americans going to start thinking for themselves and elect people that have plans and ideas that make common sense and are good for every citizen?

SECTION THREE
THINGS ABOUT PEOPLE THAT MAKE ME MAD

1. A young lady was shot in broad daylight in San Francisco, CA. while walking along the waterfront with her father. Now why does this particular murder set me off, because there are murders everyday around the world and we should be mad about them all. It's because her killer was an illegal alien and felon that was deported 5 times! The reason he was walking around free is that San Francisco is considered a "sanctuary city," whatever that's supposed to mean. To make matters worse no one would take responsibility for the man being in the country. All the local and federal authorities ever did was go on TV crying what a shame it was and pointed fingers of blame at each other.

There appears to be some type of loop-hole by which a city can ignore federal immigration laws. This provides an illegal alien "sanctuary" or protection from being deported by federal authorities. Where was this young lady's "sanctuary" or her protection from being shot down in cold blood on a public pier! Who do you point the finger of blame at for her death?

No one is going to step up and take responsibility for this and that young lady should not be dead. When are, people going to come to their senses and demand real enforcement of immigration laws that work and stop letting our government officials, local or federal, get away with their incompetence?

Now in 2021 look at what the current federal administration is doing to control illegal aliens….nothing. As a matter of fact they have stopped border control and basically told everyone in Mexico, Central and South America come on in we don't care.

Illegals are actually pouring over the border in the thousands daily. America will be destroyed from within by our own leaders and their stupid policies and actions or the lack of. We don't have a dictator, but we are acting like a third world country.

2. I hate bicycles in the roadway. In my day, we road our bikes on the sidewalks and yes in the streets, but when a car was coming, we got out of the street or moved to the curb. Today you have all these amateur bicyclists in the roadways that think they're getting ready for the Olympics. I was taught that motor vehicles have the right of way except in areas like crosswalks. Bicyclist now days believe they have the right of way over everyone, everywhere, and some cities have given them all kinds of rights over motor vehicles. I'm reasonably sure the engineers didn't figure road dimensions and pavement stress factors with bicycles in mind.

In some cities bike lanes have been added, but still there are many bicyclists that won't stay in a bike lane or they ride the white dividing stripe, still causing traffic problems. Bicycles belong anywhere except in the middle of the roadway with 2 tons of automobile bearing down on them.

Why invite disaster? Take your bikes to the track or to the country or use some common sense, pay attention and yield to motor vehicles. The streets and highways were NOT designed for pedestrians or bicycles; they were designed for motor vehicles. So, until we come up with some alternate mode of transportation that is compatible with bicycles. Don't be the cause of traffic problems or the cause of a sad and avoidable accident.

3. Respect the dead and the mourners. It is true that most states don't have traffic laws that specifically deal with funeral motorcades, but there are many traditions that are observed. Stay in line and with the procession at all times, even if means you are going through a red light at an intersection. Local traffic ordinances give a funeral procession the right-of-way, and other motorists must yield until the procession has passed. Once the lead car in the procession appropriately goes through a traffic light or stop sign, the entire procession is typically allowed to follow. Yield the right-of-way until the entire procession is through the intersection.

Never join a funeral procession by tagging onto the end or cutting into the middle of one.

There are case precedents that when people not in a funeral procession have caused an accident they were cited and fined for failure to yield or reckless driving. So the bottom line is when you see a funeral procession just stop, yield, move over or whatever is needed to allow them to safely pass. There has already been one death, don't be the cause of another.

4. When I need customer service for my TV dish, phone service, computer, or one of my credit cards, it really irritates me to call and I'm immediately greeted by a recorded voice, that really tightens my jaw. I hate phone menus and the voices on them! The first thing you hear is "thank you for calling…please listen carefully for our menu options have changed." Now a voice comes in Spanish saying "Si desea escuchar este menú en español, presione dos" or something like that and of course I ignore it.

Next you may hear "we're experiencing a higher than normal call volume, your approximate wait time will be 15 minutes, or you may press three to leave us your name, number, the nature of your call and we will return your call as soon as possible." Or you may also hear "Your call is very important to us, all calls are answered in the order they were received, please hold and a customer service representative will be with you as soon as possible."

Now you sit and wait on hold for forever listening to either the worst concert or 80's music you ever heard or terrible infomercials that have nothing to do with your problem. Then when you finally get transferred to another machine you hear "so we can better serve you and for training purposes this call may be recorded." **I Don't Care, Just Give Me Someone To Talk Too!**

No….you don't get to talk to a live breathing person yet. You must now answer questions like, "please say or enter your account number."

Then the computer wants to know your first and last name, the phone number on the account, what you are calling about, do you want to continue with the automated service and no telling what else before it transfers you to someone that will speak to you in a live voice.

It's about now that I want to hang up or just **SCREAM** into the phone, but I take a deep breath, knowing that I would only sound and look very foolish yelling at a computer-generated voice. NOW…....the topper is, after you have given all your vital information to the computer a live breathing person finally comes on the line. They can never use simple names like Frank, Jim, or Susan. They have to use names that only they can pronounce and the first thing they say is "hello my name is….For verification, my I have your name and the phone number on the account?" **AGAIN**!!! I just start counting, **ONE, TWO, THREE.**

At this point my blood pressure has reached a dangerous level, my voice has gone up a few decibels and sounds more like a woman's voice than my own. I've been on the phone pushing buttons so long that I've forgotten why I made this call in the first place, as the agent finally starts to ask relevant questions. Depending on the reason for my call why can't I have the option to choose the automated service or go straight to a live agent with no automated questions?

5. Every time I hear a car insurance commercial on TV or radio, I get mad. The audacity of those companies to say things like "accident forgiveness" or "we won't raise your rates after your first accident." We have to buy their insurance products, it's the law and if I have an accident, they have the nerve to say I'm forgiven! I don't need nor do I want their forgiveness; I want them to live up to their part of the contract that I've been paying for with my hard earned money month after month, year after year.

These companies are not hurting for money, the people running them are living very well and after all who owns or occupies most major downtown high rises or premium office space throughout your city? Its banks, lawyers, and insurance companies. What is ever other commercial you see on TV about. If they are ever hurting for money it's their own fault, not ours. We've paid them billions each year in premiums, now when we do have an "accident" it's their time to shut up and pay up.

6. It happened again. Some crazy guy went into a college classroom in Oregon and shot 9 individuals. This was a so called "gun free zone" and what was the first thing all the liberals started yelling, gun control of course? Even the President came on TV to make a statement of condolences and couldn't resist turning it into a shameful political speech for gun control.

Once again, we're starting to find out that a shooter had many warning signs, and no one said or did anything before he went over the edge. Witnesses say this guy was asking everyone what their religion was before he shot them.

I know a lot of people that believe in the right of "Constitutional Carry" or that no one should be required to get a permit or attend a firearms course. I have a little different view on the subject. I don't care if someone has a 22 cal. or a tank, it's not the weapon I'm worried about, it's the people. Should anyone be able to buy or obtain a weapon, no way.

I want to see the control on who can obtain and carry a weapon, with respect to criminal records, mental or physical inability. I don't have all the answers, but I think we need to somehow do more in ensuring that buyers are mentally and physically capable of using a rifle or handgun? Have they been through a course that teaches proper use and safety and certifies that the individual meets all requirements? Do they have a felony background?

We all have a right to protect ourselves and our families from people that intend others harm or the career criminals regardless if we're in a large city or living on some ranch miles away from anyone else. Also, I believe this is a state rights issue, not Washington, D.C. The federal government and the courts need to uphold and protect the 2nd Amendment, period.

7.   The police are under attack! More correctly just about anyone wearing a badge and a uniform of any type is under attack. Today you have idiots marching down streets yelling "Pigs in a blanket, fry'um like bacon" or "Black lives matter." Then they get all upset if you ask them don't all lives matter?

When you have people that are breaking the law and then want to challenge a police officer's authority or those that fail to listen and follow police instructions, then someone is most likely going to get hurt. It makes me so mad to hear these groups saying they are being targeted by white police officers when it's just stupid individuals making bad decisions.

Then you get the President coming on TV making stupid statements, saying how wrong the police are in their tactics or how bad the white on black violence is. But you let it be a white police officer that is shot and killed then the President is strangely silent on the matter while out playing golf. And where are the high profile black activists' fools when it's a white police officer or bystander that's killed by a black individual?

In several cases the first thing the President comments on is gun control instead of the death that just occurred. The truth of the matter is that more whites are shot by white police officers than any other group and you never hear from all the activists when that happens. The police and other first responders are there to help everyone.

Yes, there are a few bad apples in any organization, but by in large these are all dedicated men and women putting their lives on the line every day and we all need to be thankful for their sacrifices. Without them our cities would be in total chaos and from the looks of things it appears several of our cities are headed that way.

8. When I just stated that the police are under attack, that seems to be a huge understatement. During a "black lives matter" protest a sniper in downtown Dallas opened fire on police. Twelve officers and one civilian were hit, with four Dallas police officers and one DART officer dead from gunshot wounds.

Now fast forward and in Baton Rouge, LA. three more law enforcement officers are ambushed and gun down in the street by a coward. I don't understand what is wrong with people, why does the lives of one group of people matter anymore or any less than another? Why do some people believe they can break the law and then justify it with violence? I am so mad, yet so scared for our communities. Pray for the police, pray for everyone, pray that a merciful God will deliver America from this madness.

9. In the last couple of sports seasons, I've been seeing and hearing in the news about idiots that for whatever their cause or reasons are, they're refusing to salute the flag, say the pledge of allegiance, or sing the national anthem. In Florida a school district sent a paper home with the children and if the parent signed it that child didn't have to say the pledge at the beginning of class each day. Just today, February 10, 2021 I heard on the news about the owner of the Dallas Mavericks' they will just not have the National Anthem at the beginning of each game anymore and there won't be an issue about standing or kneeling. Pro sports, there overrated, over paid, and just over for me.

I'm getting sick and tired of people teaching this country's children that showing and being a patriotic American citizen is a bad thing or is something that is just out of date and has no real meaning these days. Why can't people see that it's not the object, the flag, that you're saluting or pledging allegiance to; or the words in the national anthem, but it's the nation, it's the people that it represents. **"E Pluribus Unum"** out of the many, the one. Do we not believe this anymore?

We're one nation of many different people, with many different backgrounds, talents and abilities and we have come together to form the most perfect union we can. To dedicate ourselves to the common good and to protect and defend ourselves as one nation, one country, one people. That is what the flag is about, the anthem, the pledge and if anyone is against any of this, then freedom allows you to get out and go find something better! It makes me so mad to even see them get a 30 second spot on the evening news when they deserve nothing.

10. Journalism Is In Critical Condition In America. With the exception of a few media sources, journalism and journalist in this country are seriously flawed. It used to be, find the story, investigate and gather the facts, verify sources and facts, then report it without the journalist's personal opinions, biases, or conjecture on anyone's part. I remember when the last 3 minutes of a news broadcast was left for commentary by the network or local station. In newspapers it's the editor's column. The viewers or readers were left to use their own thoughts and values to judge the story and arrive at their own conclusions.

Sadly, that is not true in today's journalism. With all the mainstream media networks, print media, online news websites and very big talk radio stations, the competition is enormous for ratings, viewers/listeners and subscribers. Large media networks and reporters are all in fierce competition with one another and the top reporters are being paid astronomical salaries and bonuses. It's natural every reporter wants to be a national "news anchor," have their own program or their own printed bi-line, so they can put their own personal spin on the topics and stories of the day.

Today it's first with the story, don't waste time on a thorough investigation or verifying the facts, we can correct anything we get wrong later or make someone prove us wrong. Every day you hear or read "Breaking News" or "This Just In" and before you know it, the reporter has told you what happen, where it happened, when it took place, and concluded all the reasons why this event has occurred. The appropriate response at that point would have been to report what happened, where it happened, when it took place, and we'll update you as we receive more facts of the story.

Reporters are too often allowed to assume facts that were not given, report fabricated or assumed information or unverified events and then draw conclusions based own their own biases. To me the most appalling type of journalism is to have an individual, group, or organization be accused, tried, and convicted by the court of public media before one receives due process of the law and the Constitution.

Instead of remaining neutral about a story it's all about presenting the story to support that media or reporter's personal or political views and convictions. If you disagree it's perceived, you are condemning them personally and not the events or facts of the story. Their only response most often is to slander you for not supporting their conclusions.

This problem is seen most often in the dozens of TV "political talk shows" on all networks. All these "talking heads" in the mainstream media are either liberal Democratic Party hacks or conservative dogmatic Republicans. Much more in the liberal media they present many of their stories with or without supporting facts and rarely discuss the pros and cons of real issues. Radio talk shows have the same problems although I believe the most followed radio talk show hosts are conservative and do a much better presentation of issues/events with supporting facts and in-depth information.

As you can tell I believe the problem with truth and honesty is pervasive throughout the industry starting in the so-called "schools of journalism" right on up to reporters, news directors, owners and yes, most of us for supporting them with our listenership, subscriptions and consuming todays style of polluted journalism. Will we ever get back to what I call pure journalistic standards and reporting? I would say never, there's too much at stake for the different organizations. Besides with the current and mostly ineffective libel laws, will the media ever be held lawfully responsible for the truth and accuracy of what they print or broadcast. No, because no lawmaker is willing to go down that road of fines, suspending broadcast licenses, or sanctions when the lawmaker's need the media to get elected, re-elected or to promulgate their own distorted issues to the public.

So, what are we to do in order to maintain a free press, but demand a more ethical and unbiased process? I don't have the answers. Try to teach and instill in everyone at an early age the importance of truth, responsibility, accountability and pride in oneself for everything you do and say. Then maybe those that grow up to be in the media industry will change it for the better. One student, one writer, one reporter, one person at a time.

11. <u>Hoarding for no reason</u>. When the Covid pandemic first started and people were told to stay at home many of them starting buying up things like toilet paper, paper plates and other paper products. You were lucky to find a half gallon of milk. There was no shortage because plants were turning out products as fast as they could, but crazy people were buying and hording much more than they needed.

There is another group of hoarders, those that must have believed the apocalypse was coming soon. Even now over a year into the pandemic, store shelves are empty of handgun and rifle ammunition. I'm told that ammo plants are working at full capacity but people know the delivery days and times to their local stores and they are camped at the front doors.

Also many "scalpers" are buying up the ammo and then selling it at greatly inflated prices out of their garage or online and of course the shipping charges are inflated also. The only ammo I've seen on the shelves is shotgun shells for 12 and 20 gauge.

For a long time I could find a handgun in the stores or online. People were buying those up no matter what the brand or the quality of the weapon. The same thing was happening as with the ammo and scalpers and of course you have all the dooms day crowd that has everything from a slingshot to a cannon.

If people would just use the brains God gave them, none of this would have happened, but instead they started panic buying and they caused the problem of any shortages in the local stores. That's another type of people that just make me red faced mad.

SECTION FOUR
FAMILY AND OUR SOCIETY TODAY

This section is about what I believe a true Biblical family should be and what raising our children should be like. What should our priorities be, our values and acceptable behaviors in our society. Sadly, it's also about the gradual societal destruction of the family unit by our government, our courts and crazy liberal special interest groups.

1. **Life's Priorities**. Everyone will establish their own personal priorities and those priorities will change over time depending on many factors such as age, current social events, family events or even our health. However, I believe that one's own values and overriding life's priorities should be:

First and always: Our Heavenly Father, who gives us everything and has provided life eternal through Jesus Christ.

Second: Family, that gives us purpose, support, and the love we need.

Third: Country, which gives us pride and unity in who we are and what we value as one nation.

Fourth: Work, which provides us a means to acquire the physical needs to sustain our daily life.

2. **A Normal Family**. As I begin this section, I must first ask the question, what is a normal family? Now days what does our society believe a family should a normal family look like, what should it be defined as? When you stop and think about all the different views there are on marriage; homosexual unions, single parent homes, blended families and adoptions; then defining what a family is by today's societal views can be a huge task. And those views are constantly undergoing change as societies change their moral views and are more accepting to any new secular lifestyle.

The Merriam-Webster Online Dictionary has several definitions attached to the meaning of a modern Family, these being two of them: "the basic unit in society traditionally consisting of two parents rearing their children;" "also: any of various social units differing from but regarded as equivalent to the traditional family." [5] Does this second definition imply that society or I can determine for myself what a "family unit" can be?

The Bible teaches that the family is of divine origin and purpose. The Bible also provides guidelines for good relations within the family. My definition, and I believe GOD's design for the family unit as it's proclaimed in the Bible is: One man, one woman, and their offspring. Now of course "families" have always consisted of many members and includes the extended family of relatives by blood, marriage, or adoption, such as grandparents, nieces, nephews, cousins, aunts, and uncles.

The family isn't an idea born of man, but instead was created by GOD, and man has been given the responsibility of stewardship over it. GOD created man and woman, and it was GOD that ordained the union of one man and one woman for companionship and reproduction. The husband and wife are responsible for holding the marriage and the family together, despite the current sociality attitudes and opinions.

Gen. 2:24 "Therefore shall a man leave his father and his mother, and shall cleave unto his wife, and they shall be one flesh."

Sexuality expressed according to Biblical standards is a very beautiful expression of love and commitment. Outside of marriage it's sin, and GOD cannot look upon or condone sin. It would seem that our society is willing to overlook the sin and would say that a family is whatever you want to make it; that no one, including GOD, the church or the government has the right to tell you any differently. I believe that GOD has commanded that in marriage the husband and wife are to remain faithful to one another for a lifetime.

To me this Biblical truth eliminates today's popular view that divorce on demand, living together without being married, and same-sex marriage are acceptable lifestyles to a Holy GOD. On the contrary they are sin and an abomination in the sight of GOD.

Heb. 13:4 "Marriage should be honored by all, and the marriage bed kept pure, for God will judge the adulterer and all the sexually immoral." [6]

Matt. 19:6 "So then, they are no longer two but one flesh. Therefore what God has joined together, let not man separate." [7]

3. <u>**What makes us good parents**</u>?   I don't know, I can only tell you what I think good parents should do.   First, I believe good parenting involves both a father and a mother and that their marriage be grounded in their faith in Jesus Christ. Second, children are a gift from GOD, so they should be thought of as a precious responsibility. Third, raising children requires love, time, involvement, care, communication, commitments and many other verbs and adjectives I can't think of. You can't just put a child in a room with some toys, in front of a TV or a computer and expect them to grow up on their own, it doesn't work that way. You must be fully vested and involved in every aspect of a child's life.

I also believe one of the most important things a parent and don't leave out grandparents, need to learn is how and when to say "no." Saying yes and giving your child everything they want is wrong and very dangerous. Just as in every aspect of life there must be limits to what a child is allowed to do or to have, so you've got to know when to say no.

I've noticed that in today's American society there are too many parents that want to be their children's best buddy when they reach a certain age. As parents, I believe we have an obligation to spend time with our children and direct them as they grow and mature, but kids can always find buddies at school, church or in the neighborhood.

What they need most of all is parents to be parents, providers of a stable two parent home life, teachers, counselors, and disciplinarians. I love my children, but I'm still the parent and the grandparent and I always will be. My duties don't end until God calls me home.

It's absolutely amazing to look back and see how families and raising children has changed just in my lifetime and I bet just about every generation can make that same statement. We all look at how we've changed socially and how our everyday lives have been transformed by technology, medicines and education and even political policies.

When I was growing up my parents were the final authority on everything, but in today's society there are so many outside "experts" telling parents what they can and can't do with respect to raising their own children. In today's courts, kids are being given rights by liberal judges over their parents or allowed to even sue their parents for certain rights or privileges.

In 1996 Hillary Clinton wrote a book titled "It Takes a Village" and since I attach no trust to Mrs. Clinton and I have not nor dare not read this book, I will refrain from making any personal comments on it. There was a firestorm of criticism all over the country on her views of what was the proper way to raise children in a "state" environment. Former Kansas Senator Bob Dole commented "We are told that it takes a village, that is, a collective, and thus the state, to raise a child," Dole said. "And, with all due respect, I am here to tell you it does not take a village to raise a child. It takes a family to raise a child." [8]

It would appear to me that many liberals believe that instead of parents it's the "state" that knows best what should be done and how to raise our children. It's socialism and political correctness out of control. It is the liberals way of instilling their philosophy in our children from the beginning of their lives. How much better we would be if government officials would concentrate on their jobs and leave family business to families. GOD save us from them and save the family.

"My father used to play with my brother and me in the yard. Mother would come out and say, You're tearing up the grass; We're not raising grass, Dad would reply. We're raising boys." Harmon Killebrew [9]

4. <u>**HEROES**</u>. The word "Hero" as defined by the Merriam-Webster Dictionary: "a person who is admired for great or brave acts or fine qualities; a person who is greatly admired." [10]

It goes without saying that I believe our men and women in military uniform are heroes and most of the time when someone talks about a hero it's in reference to someone serving in the military. Having had the privilege to train and lead men and women in the Navy, in no way do I wish to minimize the importance and contributions by our citizens in military uniform, but in this case, I submit that many of our day to day heroes are the people we see around us all the time.

The police officers and firefighters that protect us with their skills and at times their lives. Teachers that truly love children and give many hours to inspire learning. Those in the medical fields that put in countless hours into education, training, and care for us when we're sick or injured. Look at our Ministers, leading and teaching us in what God wants for our lives. And when something happens no matter what the hour, they're always willing to counsel and comfort us in times of sickness or distress.

All of these people that I just mentioned are to be commended and praised for their time and sacrifices over the past year of 2020 and into 2021. They have worked sometimes around the clock to perform their normal duties and now with the added pandemic to give aid and care for those that have been infected with the Coronavirus, placing themselves and families in danger of exposure.

How about the parent that for whatever reason is working two or even three jobs, sacrificing their time in order to provide food and shelter for their children? And no one can forget the stay at home parent that spends 16 hours a day cooking, cleaning, washing, running errands all over the city and in times of sickness comforting the ones they love.

Heroes come to us from every part of our lives and are around us every day. I believe they all deserve our praise and admiration. They do what they are called to do because they love it and love the ones they serve. Tell someone in your life today and every day that you appreciate what they do and that they are a real life HERO to you.

5. **<u>Why do some marriages last</u>**? The beloved and trusted long time Chicago radio host Paul Harvey had a feature on his daily show that highlighted couples that had been married for 50 years or more and those who had reached their 100th birthday. I loved his reports and stories so much and tried never to miss them.

As of August 2021, my wife and I will celebrate 49 years of marriage and I'm often asked by younger folks how did we make it last so long? I think my first response is "I married my best friend" and then they look at me with either a delightful understanding smile, or a very puzzled and confused expression.

I'll admit that when we first met it was a physical attraction, but as we began to spend time together, she became my best friend. I don't think I realized I truly loved her until we had our first child. Then as I stood beside a hospital bed as a new and very scared father and gazed down at my young wife and at a small baby, it hit me, not in the head, but in the heart. Now of course looking back 49 years later it's much easier to see and understand and that she was the one that GOD intended for me, for a lifetime. Most of us guys are too short sighted and don't see that fact in the beginning.

What does this story have to do with Family & Children? If you heard Paul Harvey talk about his wife Lynne, who he always called Angel, and those couples on his radio broadcast you could tell that they truly loved each other and they were totally committed to each other and to those around them, their family. It wasn't something that just happened but was a relationship that had to be strong and most of all had a solid foundation based on their mutual faith in GOD, His commandments and in each other.

6. **<u>Was it easier to grow up in my generation</u>**? When I was growing up in the 1950's and 60's we had the freedom to play all over our neighborhood, just respect other families' property and be home for lunch and dinner. Dad was at work and Mom was in the house doing her daily chores. Most of the time it was the classic "Leave it to Beaver" neighborhoods we lived in and we weren't always in site of a parent.

Today it would be child endangerment to let your seven or eight-year-old child go across the street and play on the playground equipment without a parent being within ten feet of that child. But I must say that in some cities or neighborhoods that would be dangerous not to have a parent nearby. Why is that? Have we become such a depraved society that we can't trust each other with the lives of our children?

Kids are going to get cuts and bruises or even break some bones with or without a parent nearby, that's just a fact of life. My fear is why do I have to be so concerned about what another adults might do to my child who is just out playing? Has that fear always been there, and we just hear more about it these days? Maybe the real fear needs to be what will happen to anyone that intentionally harms or abuses any child. Maybe we need better laws and courts with judges that say there is no "first time offence," there is only "one offence" and your gone, there will be no second chance to harm a child.

7. **<u>Mind your manners</u>**! Shame on us as parents and grandparents for not exhibiting and teaching our children common manners, etiquette, and respect. I don't understand why this is so hard to do. How often do you hear a "yes sir" or a "no ma'am" when your children speak to you or

another adult? Have you ever seen a gentleman hold the chair for a woman in a restaurant? Do you remember when a man would open or close the car door for a woman? How about, don't interrupt when someone else is speaking, it's considered to be selfish and ill-mannered, wait for your turn. It makes me want to scream "shut your mouth" when I hear people all talking at the same time and they have no idea what the other person is saying.

Here's one that really gets me, sitting down to the dinner table, at home or at a restaurant, with your hat on! There was a time when you just might get your hat and your head handed to you if you disrespected your father's or grandfather's table like that. Parents you will enjoy that meal just as much without your ball cap or your ten-gallon cowboy hat on your head! Oh, yea and teach your kids that you don't just sit down and start eating until everyone has been seated, served, and grace has been offered.

There are 5 rules of proper cowboy hat (and I include ballcaps) etiquette and the first rule is "Know When to Remove Your Hat. During the National Anthem, Pledge of Allegiance, the passing of the flag, in church, during prayer, and during a funeral procession -- all require the hat to go. Also, remove your hat when introduced to a woman. You can hold the hat in one hand while you shake her hand in greeting with the other. Last but not least, remove your hat when entering a building or private home, when you begin a new conversation, dining in a restaurant, or when speaking with an elder of the church. Basically, just plan on not wearing hats indoors as a good rule of thumb."[11]

Many people blame the "Cowboy Churches" for the past couple of decades of bad etiquette when it comes to the hat. Many of them allow attendees to enter the church and keep their hat on during service with the exception of during the Lord's Prayer or during the observance of the Lord's Supper. I once walked into the church sanctuary before the service with one of my ballcaps on and it wasn't intentional, I just forgot I had it on. Well one of the elderly ladies gave me "the look" and asked, "is your head cold?" I didn't make that mistake again.

Back on the subject of eating and specifically going out to a restaurant I get so disgusted with how people of all ages dress when they go out in public. Not long ago my wife and I were at a wedding and stopped at a restaurant on the way home. Of course, we were dressed nicely, but as I sat there waiting for our dinners, I began to notice how people were "undressed."

This was not a 5-Star restaurant, but it was a nice family place. There were men and women wearing ragged cut off's and T-shirts displaying inappropriate language for any age. One young woman had very short, shorts on that revealed large dagger tattoos that were hard to miss on each outer thigh. Of course, just about every other person that came in had tattoos visible somewhere on their body. Just like I said above, hats of all kinds on or if the men didn't have one on, their hair looked like it hadn't been combed in a week. Women with their hair unkept or up in a ball so they didn't have to comb or fix it.

I call this the Wal-Mart generation. Nothing against Wal-Mart, they're a great store and I shop there all the time, it's just that people think it's okay to go there in their PJ's or even less. Lord what ever happen to people putting on nice, clean and appropriate clothing when they go out in public? Overseas in Europe I would see women wearing dresses just to go down to the local market. Men wore nice pants and collared shirts, and parents dressed their children up in very nice outfits. It's not a matter of being comfortable, it's just that so many people now days have no self-respect. They don't care what other people think of them, because they don't even care about themselves.

A few years back my wife and I were fortunate to travel to Istanbul, Turkey to see our daughter and her family who are missionaries. One evening we were introduced to two young boys that were quests in my daughter's home. I was surprised when the boys bowed in front of me and then placed my hand on their forehead in a sign of respect. Later I noticed when we were using public trains or busses that males always showed respect by offering their seats to any woman or any man that was their elder, which really impressed me. They even did it to me.

Let me add this last item, cell phones! I could write a whole book on things I consider to be bad manners involving the use of cell phones. Of course, never use your cell phone while driving. Don't try to talk to me while your attention is really on your phone and never sit at the dinner table and continuously text or play games on your phone. Many people, including me, consider that type of behavior to be very rude and selfish. Try having an old fashioned conversation with the people you are with, you just might enjoy it, if you remember how.

"A child who is allowed to be disrespectful to his parents will not have true respect for anyone." Billy Graham [12]

8. <u>**Are we educating or indoctrinating our children**</u>? I was surfing through the radio channels in my vehicle one day and a conversation on one of the talk radio stations caught my ear. They were discussing our education system. One person described our public schools and colleges, as "a place of indoctrination, not education" and I agreed.

In my humble opinion it appears that in all of the Texas school districts children are only being taught the information required to pass the state standardized exams. These exams are intended to measure academic achievement across multiple disciplines and several grade levels, but to me they serve absolutely no academic purpose in their current application. The only results I see are how well students memorized information presented by teachers in order to achieve a passing score.

In Texas, I've now heard reports that more school districts are considering connecting a teacher's pay raise to how well their students do on the statewide exams. So, focusing only on that, all the teacher instructs their students on is the test material instead of being free to really teach them how to think.

From year to year if the majority of the test scores fall below the desired benchmark then officials lower those marks in order to show that our children are being educated properly, but they're not, instead it's what we call "dumbing down" the scores and required information. So, I really don't believe that our system has improved any.

Our children are not being taught complicated math, how to read and write at a high school or college level. "According to the U.S. Department of Education, 54% of adults between 16-74 years old - about 130 million people - lack proficiency in literacy, reading below the equivalent of a sixth-grade level." [13] No one is teaching them how to look at history or today's society and to apply critical thinking.

When I was stationed at the Naval Air Station in Meridian, MS., I recall a person saying that for Mississippi schools to move up the ranking of nationwide school systems they would have to make Puerto Rico the 51st state. How sad is that? Well Mississippian's now in 2021 the Democrats are looking at making Puerto Rico and the District of Columbia new states. I guess the poverty level would put Puerto Rico's educational level below Mississippi and the District of Columbia would then be last because of all the stupid people we send there from the current 50 states.

There is nothing new about parents "home schooling" their children, it's been done for centuries, except that in today's society it's much more organized. I wasn't a fan of it years ago, but my opinion has changed a lot as our educational system has continued to spiral downward over the years and come under more criticism. In order to turn our school systems around I say one of our first steps is do away with standardized tests and let teachers go back to what teachers are supposed to do, provide information, provide instruction, instill creative thinking, in other words, TEACH. One other thing, stop rewriting text books so they reflect today's "political correctness."

Next and just as important, I believe we must rid our nation of the National Education Association (NEA). It's the largest labor union in the United States with over 3 million members. The NEA holds a Congressional charter and was founded in Philadelphia in 1857. The stated mission of the NEA is: "to advocate **for education professionals** and to unite our members and the nation to fulfill the promise of public education to prepare every student to succeed in a diverse and interdependent world."[14] In other words, the organization itself is first priority.

The NEA is a non-profit tax-exempt labor organization and should be a non-partisan organization, but it typically supports Democratic Party candidates. State affiliates of the NEA routinely lobby state legislators for funding, seek to influence education policy, and file legal actions.

"At the national level, the NEA lobbies Congress and federal agencies and is active in the nominating process for Democratic candidates. From 1989 through the 2014 election cycle, the NEA spent over $92 million on political campaign contributions, 97% of which went to Democrats."[15]

"The NEA's proposed budget boosts it's president's base salary from $311,138 to $320,783 (although federal reports reveal the actual compensation is $429,569) and offers similar raises to the union's vice president and secretary-treasurer over the next two years."[16] As far as I'm concerned the NEA is an illegal arm of the Democrat Party. They should have no political affiliation and should be prosecuted for any political contributions or influence peddling over our representatives and the election process.

Let's end this century and a half of insanity and free our teachers from all the rules and restrictions of such an oppressive organization and an over-reaching federal government. Let's give teaching back to our states, back to our local communities, the classroom teacher, and the parents. Let's restore the joy of learning back to the children and make our local schools a place of education, not indoctrination. Let's make all of our schools a place of pride for the whole community. Let's make our children first priority, not the NEA labor union hacks!

9. <u>**My opinion on Home Schooling**</u>. I just briefly mentioned "home schooling" and that my opinion of it has changed over the years. I see that many children have received a fine education that has prepared them for college or for entering the workforce. My brother and his wife did it, my sister, and all three of my children have all chosen home schooling for their children.

At first, I thought they were all going to really hurt their children's education, but it can be very beneficial if both parents are fully committed, involved in the process and the primary teaching parent is organized.

The home schooling co-ops that have been established in so many communities can be very beneficial to the parent and the children. My only reservation with home schooling is the lack of "social interaction" in some cases. To me this is something that is a very important part of children's maturity and growing process.

Knowing how to interact with other children and other adults is also a skill we must learn early in life and that can't be done if you never get out of your own home. Children that are also very active in church, scouting or athletic programs and even the home school co-ops I believe will receive a well-rounded education.

10. <u>**"Time Out."**</u> Now what is that and how will it instill any kind of discipline in a child? In daily life, can you just call a "time out" when you have done something wrong, or you don't like something that is happening? Will your employer sit you in a corner when you haven't completed your work or maybe it doesn't meet company standards? A mad or upset parent may need to take a "time out" before they react to a child's behavior, but otherwise the parent must step up and immediately deal with whatever the problem is with their child.

A child must learn and learn early that there are always consequences for their actions or behavior whether it's good or bad. That doesn't include putting the child in a corner or sent to their room and told something like "now you just think about what you did" or maybe "you sit there until you're ready to do what I told you." That's not discipline, that's just a few convenient moments for the parent. Also if you think the child is going to do either one of those things your dreaming. That child is thinking about something else or maybe I've got a few minutes that I'm not being yelled at.

Parents don't need to talk in a childish tone of voice either, use your own stern voice. Yelling, I know we have all done it, but it's stupid. All yelling does is put the parent on display as an out of control person. A stern, normal tone of voice will do, because the lesson to the child needs to be that you will follow through with your discipline.

I've heard that now days in military boot camp (if it's still going on) you can call a "time out" if the instructor is yelling and upsetting you or if the pace of things is just getting too stressful. Will that work in training or in actual combat? I can just hear some Gomer Pile out on a training exercise or in the battlefield yelling "Time out, time out, don't shoot."

This must be one of the dumbest, stupidest, mind numbing things I have ever heard in raising children or training our military forces. When are we going to stop listening to these idiot liberals and get back to disciplining/teaching our children that a person must take responsibility for all their own actions?

11. <u>What are the really important things in school</u>? Years ago I was privileged to watch one of my grandsons sing with his school choir at the Bass Performance Hall in downtown Fort Worth. My wife and I really enjoyed the presentation very much, but something disturbed me. The superintendent of the district had a few words about the district's fine arts programs. He praised the programs, and everyone involved while telling us how much emphasis the district puts on them; how many awards are won annually; and how important these programs are to the children and their growth.

As I listened, I didn't disagree with anything he was saying, the speech was appropriate for the occasion. But I thought with all the public schools in this country doing so poorly, with the growing home school movement, maybe their strongest emphasis should be placed elsewhere. Where was the emphasis on the things that you need for college, for business, and everyday life? Just where are our priorities in the public school systems?

I don't believe it's the things we need. To use an analogy I think they are being taught step by step processes or "paint by the numbers" not how to use critical or independent thinking. Are we really emphasizing and teaching them what it will take to be successful in tomorrow's world?

12. <u>No Winners, No Losers.</u> At some point there must have been a meeting of parents, coaches and teachers that came up with the idea that in any competition there should not be winners or losers declared. The reason being that it falsely builds up the winners to believing they are better than anyone else and it could hurt the feelings or damage the losers self-esteem. So in their wisdom it was decided that in many youth sports and other city and school competitions there would be no winners and no losers declared. Also no trophies would be awarded, or there would be "Participation" trophies awarded to all the youth.

Well I'm sorry little children, but neither child or adult life is like that and you're in for a rude awakening. In life there are always winners and losers in sports and every other aspect of human life. People lose relationships, jobs, and advancements. We even lose our health, and we lose people we love to someone else or in their passing. Everyone will suffer loss many times in their lives and it starts when they are young. If we are not teaching and showing our children how to properly deal with it at an early age that child can or will have trouble later in life.

If you lose a game you train harder, you try harder the next time and the next, and the next. If you lose a job you don't just give up, you do what it takes to get the job the next time. If you lose a relationship, don't cry and give up, move on and tell yourself you can do better next time.

Adults don't shelter your children on this issue. Teach them there are winners and losers in life and teach them how to deal with both. Life isn't fair and it doesn't hand out "Participation" trophies for just showing up. Parents don't handicap your children by teaching them this politically correct lie.

13. **<u>Are you addicted or is it OCD</u>**?   Do you have a problem not being able to put down any of your electronic devices? I think one of the biggest problems facing people of all ages is the obsession with electronic devices. I have no problem with the advancements we've made and how they've made our daily lives more efficient and more enjoyable. If I didn't have this computer, I might not even be writing this book, but I'm not going to spend my entire day in front of it.

I see the biggest problem with many people is not being able to put down your smart phones, because there is almost nothing you can't do on them. Talk, send email/messages, play games and my phone has one of the best cameras I've ever had on it. Believe it or not the commonly used term for this condition is "no·mo·pho·bia" meaning "fear of being without access to a working cell phone." [17]   Yes, it's a real term and I wish I could take credit for it, but I didn't make it up.

Also, "According to University of Arkansas researchers, the use of cell phones while driving may be linked to obsessive-compulsive disorder (OCD) traits instead of an addiction, which commonly had been named the culprit in this dangerous behavior." [18] Common indicators of an OCD personality in cell phone usage in dangerous situations or in inappropriate places are, I answer or make calls/text messages/emails while driving. I don't care how good of a driver you think you are, no one is good enough to drive and text at the same time. Don't be one of the approximately 3,000 drivers killed each year because of "distracted driving."

Also a compulsion to check your phone without regard to where you are or using your phone in inappropriate places like in church or in a movie theater. How about, what do you think when you sit down to dinner after a busy day, and all you want to do is have a conversation with your loved ones and all they seem to want to do is text or surf on their phone? Please enjoy all the great devices that research and technology has provided us, but use them responsibly, give your loved ones more time than you give your phone.

14. <u>Growing Old</u>: Why do writers often talk about grumpy old men and even make a movie with the same title. I've suddenly realized that with each passing year my emotions show themselves more and more. It's sometimes hard to keep them in check. I get mad easier when I see people doing something that I consider to be dumb. My mouth and my emotions get ahead of my brain and I end up saying things that only a few years ago I would have just kept to myself.

With my children and grandchildren I watch them go about their everyday lives or accomplish some small task and I tear up with love and pride. I watch some TV show like "The Voice" and I cry when someone sings a beautiful song. I watch "M.A.S.H." a comedy show, and I laugh one moment and cry the next when they show the real horrors of war without saying a word.

I once sang in church choirs, but now my voice cracks with emotion and I cry when singing Rock of Ages. I guess when you get older God reveals Himself to some in a much more tender way with the things that have greater meaning.

SECTION FIVE
"WE THE PEOPLE," DEFENDING FREEDOM

This section includes with a few quotes that I think need to be remembered. Also, there are issues of a historical nature, but are still relevant today and some of my thoughts about our military and how they are deployed and utilized around the globe.

1. **<u>Are you a proud American</u>**?   As I write this entry, it's the 4th of July and the birthday of our nation and many headlines around the country today and in the past read something like "What does it mean to be a proud American." First what did our founding fathers believe it meant to be an "American?" What did they believe so deeply in, that it was worth starting a revolution and to risk the lives of their families and themselves? I believe all you need to do is look at their words in many of their writings and the words of the American Declaration of Independence:

"We hold these truths to be self-evident, that all men are created equal, that they are endowed by their Creator with certain unalienable Rights that among these are Life, Liberty, and the pursuit of Happiness." [19]

In America today is there evidence that all men are not just "created equal," but in fact they are treated equally by all elements of our society and by their fellow citizens? How is the plight of the poor and the interests of the wealthy looked upon and treated by those with the power over us? As fellow citizens, do we treat or judge each other by the content of our character and not by the color of our skin, our religion, or our national origin, the dream of Martin Luther King?

Since our country's beginning I believe we have made great strides in ethnic equality and improving or overcoming our racial intolerance, but it's still a problem for everyone. I see that we are losing many of our individual rights. With an ever increasingly intrusive federal government, I believe that we are incrementally losing many of our liberty's that allow us to live as a truly free nation.

Our pursuit of happiness is increasingly constricted by an overbearing and overreaching government passing laws and restrictions that erode the very document that our government once held so dear. It would sometime seem that the legislator's only purpose is to procure tax dollars for their individual home districts or secure political power for future use instead of fulfilling their oath to protect and defend the Constitution of the United States.

"That to secure these rights, Governments are instituted among Men, deriving their just powers from the consent of the governed." [20]

We the people of this nation, the "governed" once elected the majority of our government officials that held those "just powers," but government has grown much larger than our founding fathers could have ever envisioned. Now we have unknown numbers of unelected "appointees" and their staffs that enjoy those "just powers" over our lives and we have very little, if any, recourse to reduce their influence and power.

I learned recently there are over 4,000 appointed positions within the federal system that the president gets to appoint when they're empty. If you don't think so then tell me who elected those in the Departments of Energy, Homeland Security, Treasury, or Justice. How about EPA, FBI, IRS, the Federal Reserve and Federal Judges on the Supreme Court and across the country. They're all political appointees that we the people never had a choice.

There are staggering numbers of federal and state departments, agencies and commissions that have the "just powers" to affect our daily lives without the consent of the "governed." By the power of law these appointees have the authority to seize your assets, your property, your very freedom, all before you receive due process of the law and the courts. They can ruin your business, your very life before you realize what's happening.

The law and the courts, how about the nine individuals in black robes that sit on the highest court in the country? These "appointees" are the third branch of our government and can exercise great power over our lives based solely on their individual moral character, beliefs, and judgements.

If these justices truly interpreted ours laws and controversies against the Constitution and that all Americans received equal justice that would be great. However, these are people that come to the court with a lifetime of their own personal beliefs, established political positions and differing ideologies. Can they ignore all of that and focus on strict interpretations of the Constitution and the cases that come before them?

Their individual or collective decisions can have life and death results. Their judgements will affect all our lives, now and well into the future. And now in 2021 the Democrat Party wants the new President and the Congress to "Pack the Court" by appointing at least two more liberal justices.

It's the purpose of government to secure and protect our GOD given rights that the founding generation declared to be, Life, Liberty, and the Pursuit of Happiness.   It's not the purpose of government to become the grantor of these rights. Today our government officials along with hundreds of unelected officials now believe the government structure is the best vessel in which to grant and control our GOD given freedoms and that the government knows best what will make us safe and happy.

"That whenever any Form of Government becomes destructive of these ends, it's the Right of the People to alter or to abolish it, and to institute new Government, laying its foundation on such principles and organizing its powers in such form, as to them shall seem most likely to affect their Safety and Happiness." [21]

The federal government has taken control of private companies, seized private and public lands, and now controls several industries in our nation, the most recent one being the health care industry. The federal government passes laws to aid and protect the public at large, but over time these laws allow the government to gain increasingly more control.

As the Constitution declares when a government becomes destructive it's the right of the people and I believe our duty, to alter or abolish it and lay the foundation for a new government, but the question is, how? The first and civil response would be to elect people that believe the way you do. This might be good at the local level and for the short run at the state level, but you still have a bloated and overbearing federal system with all the regulations that nobody can keep track of. So, is it time for some form of revolution?

I think so, but what would that revolution look like? Certainly, we don't want a 1776 form of revolution, besides who would we be fighting. You certainly don't want states trying to secede from the Union as in 1860. A divided America could not stand against the strong political influences and military forces of other world superpowers.

So, the problems still remain, how do we scale back the powers "we the people" have allowed our various levels of government to gain? How do "we the people" restrict the powers of unelected officials over our rights as American citizens? How do "we the people" regain our individual rights and the rights known as "States Rights?" How do "we the people" effect the reduction of the size and power of our federal system outside those enumerated by our Constitution? How do "we the people" scale back the out of control spending of our tax dollars for federal programs and projects that we either don't need or that should be the concern of the states. My answer would be a Constitutional Convention.

Article V: United States Constitution

"The Congress, whenever two thirds of both houses shall deem it necessary, shall propose amendments to this Constitution, or, on the application of the legislatures of two thirds of the several states, shall call a convention for proposing amendments, which, in either case, shall be valid to all intents and purposes, as part of this Constitution, when ratified by the legislatures of three fourths of the several states, or by conventions in three fourths thereof, as the one or the other mode of ratification may be proposed by the Congress;" [22]

A group called the Convention of States (COS) has been working on getting a Constitutional Convention called through the state legislatures based on three issues: "limiting the federal government's powers, restraining fiscal spending, and establishing term limits for members of Congress and other federal elected officials." [23]   This would be a monumental moment in the history of our country, and we would move forward as a nation.

Will "we the people" continue to allow the erosion of our freedoms and the dreams that this country's founding fathers had of a "government of the people, by the people and for the people." Will we as the heirs of this great nation toss it aside in such a caviler manner, disrespecting the sacrifices of so many patriots that gave so much?

Back to the original question, "What does it mean to be a proud American?" Without question, this is still the greatest nation on earth and it's incumbent on "we the people" to stay involved with the process of protecting our freedoms and that every citizen makes their voices heard by their vote, their service, and the way we live our daily lives. But despite all the negative things I have said I'm still proud to be an American.

Proud of the freedoms we still enjoy and the right to express our opinions about our government and our elected officials. I'm free to do what I'm doing right now, writing my thoughts and opinions without the fear of reprisal by a tyrannical dictator or a heavy handed government that fears an empowered populous. So, on every 4th of July celebrate the birth of one of the greatest nations ever created and blessed by our Heavenly Father, remember those that gave it to us and celebrate freedom.

2.   <u>What kind of tax</u>?   I've already mentioned Boston Minister Jonathan Mayhew who used the term "No taxation without representation" in one of his sermons over two decades before the war of independence began. In today's America are we overtaxed, is there too much government to support or is everything as it should be?

Rev. Mayhew would roll over in his grave if he knew of all the different taxes we have today. Federal income tax, State income tax, payroll tax, sales tax, gas tax, import tax, export tax, property tax, school tax, hospital district tax, capital gains tax, corporate tax, gift tax, inheritance tax, untold numbers of fees and tariffs, and even the stupid death tax. There are all kinds of others that I don't even know or can think of right now.

Every election cycle taxes are a big issue, and the Politian's all talk about them and make all kinds of promises about lowering taxes on the middle class or eliminating some taxes all together. Of course, it never happens, because if they did how would they fund our over bloated and ever increasing size of government. So many people have talked about doing away with the IRS as it exists today and replacing our payroll and federal income tax with something much simpler.

In my opinion I believe we are overtaxed, but first we must reduce the size of government. Once un-needed agencies and programs are eliminated then you can reduce the amount of taxes needed to run the government. As far as the IRS is concerned, I believe that agency has over the years gained too much power to the point that it almost operates as a fourth branch of government, independent of the constitution.

I believe it's time to scrap the IRS and come up with a new tax system. I would accept some type of earnings tax that is paid up front like we do now with our payroll withholdings. However, there would be no annual filing, because the government has already received what they are entitled to. Additionally, there might be a very limited sales tax on consumer products, but most other taxes have to be eliminated. The government has no right to our savings, investments, inheritance, or property now or at the time of our death. We are in desperate need of tax reform.

3. <u>**"Taking Chance."**</u> This is a movie about the trip home for a fallen marine and the LtCol. that escorted his body home. It's based on a true story and I had seen it once a couple of years ago, but I decided to watch it again and I'm glad I did. This time I noticed little things in it that to me had great meaning.

Kevin Bacon stars as LtCol. Michael Strobl who volunteers to escort the body of 19 year old Lance Corporal, Chance Phelps, because they are both from the same hometown in Colorado. Phelps was killed in action in Iraq, but before the trip home begins Strobl learns that the Corporal's family now lives in Dubois, Wyoming, where they want him laid to rest.

Strobl is fighting his own guilt for taking a desk job instead of leading men in combat because he wanted to come home and see his family every night. Later an old Korean War Vet admonishes Strobl for feeling sorry for himself, telling Strobl that "someone must remain here to bear witness to those that have fallen, or they are just forgotten."

The movie shows how Strobl comes to understand those words and that there is honor and respect in every role in the military including what he has volunteered to do. It's very heartwarming to see how everyday people from those that prepared the body to those in the airport and airlines that transported the remains and LtCol. Strobl to their destination show respect and gratitude.

It was a very emotional movie for me, because during my own Navy career I have had the unfortunate duty to be the one notifying a parent that their child had been killed. I have also presented the flag at a funeral, including my own father's funeral and believe me it's not an easy thing to do. "On behalf of the President of the United States, the United States Air

Force, and a grateful Nation, please accept this flag as a symbol of our appreciation for your loved one's honorable and faithful service."

When I said those words to my mother I felt as if someone had just kick me in the gut. Also, I have had to notify a mother with "I regret to inform you that your son………was killed in action during…" These are two of the most gut wrenching statements you will ever hear or have to make and the man that can say them without emotion or pain has no understanding of their meaning.

I strongly recommend that you watch the movie. Regardless of how many liberties Hollywood took with the story you will have a new understanding of this nations citizens that take on the duty of military service.

4. <u>Does America have the will to win</u>? As America starts to withdraw our troops from around the world, I had a few thoughts about our military. I spent 26 years in the Navy and everything I learned and trained to do was geared towards being the best fighting force we could. It was about going to war against any enemy of the United States or our allies, so I think I know a couple of things about a military force and how they are supposed to be deployed and utilized.

Ever since the end of WWII we have failed to finish every major military conflict that we became involved in. In Korea, we called it a United Nations Police Action and the battle was a stalemate and we have kept troops on the border of North and South Korea for over 65 years.

Other than individuals from all over America I don't remember reading about the New York, Chicago, or any other police department being deployed over there. It was young men and women in military uniforms from many different countries that bleed and died in that WAR. The only military police action is on a military base or those deployed in a combat roll.

We got our rear ends kicked out of South Vietnam, because politicians ran the war for political reasons back in Washington instead of the military commanders in the field. The politicians were so worried about what China or Russia might do they didn't dare turn the military commanders loose and actually let them properly fight the war. Instead politicians' were primarily focused on the politics of war, their careers and how it played out on the evening news, but not with the lives of solders and citizens on all sides.

By most standards Kuwait was just a skirmish and the lead-in to the war with Iraq. In Iraq we won the conflict, but the important issue is, we need to follow through after the victory and ensure the rights of the people to start and maintain a new government, to rebuild their infrastructure, to have free elections and now guard against extremists or another dictator taking over the country.

At the time of this book we are still in Afghanistan after 20 years having suffered 2,420 combat deaths thus far. That may not seem like very many over a 20 year period, but my biggest question is, why are we still there? As far as I'm concerned this is Washington politics keeping soldiers from doing what they were trained and capable of doing. There is no justifiable reason for having been there this long.

Some amateur historians may say remember the victories in the Cuban Missile Crises, Panama, Libya or how about Kuwait. While these were very important historical events that affected many people in their respective countries, they were not long protracted conflicts that would change the governments in that region or the world like other wars down through history have done.

It's the constitutional responsibility of our government to provide for the common defense against all enemies foreign and domestic and when in the course of world events that our life, liberty or property is being threatened here or on the shores of one of our allies, it's the constitutional duty and moral responsibility of our government to act in our common defense. It's therefore imperative that our military forces, active, reserve, and National Guard units all remain strong, trained and ready to fight on a moment's notice in any region on the globe.

If you're going to be a global power, if you're going to sign treaties and promise to assist and defend your allies you better act like a global power. You cannot "downsize" your military forces or let your equipment become old or obsolete in times of peace. Times of peace are followed immediately by conflict and you can't raise a military fighting force overnight. People must be trained; ships, planes and other implements of war get old and out of date and must be renewed or replaced. It would seem to me that our civilian and military leaders have forgotten what a military force is for or how to properly train and deploy them in a combat environment.

Like in most activities of life there are rules, such as in sports, traffic rules, business rules and ethics, and yes there are "the rules of war, or international humanitarian law (as it is known formally) are a set of international rules that set out what can and cannot be done during an armed conflict.

As out of place as it may seem the main purpose of international humanitarian law (IHL) is to maintain some humanity in armed conflicts, saving lives and reducing suffering. In order to do that, IHL regulates how wars are fought, balancing two aspects: weakening the enemy and limiting suffering.

The rules of war are universal. The Geneva Conventions (which are the core element of IHL) have been ratified by all 195 states. Very few international treaties have this level of support. Everyone fighting a war needs to respect IHL, both governmental forces and non-State armed groups.

If the rules of war are broken, there are consequences. War crimes are documented and investigated by States and international courts. Individuals can and have been prosecuted for war crimes." [24] Now you have what I call the "Roberts' Rules of War." The following are those rules of war.

Rule One:

Negotiate (with a determined and prayerful attitude)

Rule Two:

When negotiations with a foreign aggressor have failed and an armed conflict appears to be the only recourse, the Commander-in-Chief shall advise or obtain from Congress their concurrence to use military force or obtain a Declaration of War.

Rule Three:

Having received Congressional approval, it's now the Congress' obligation to continue to provide adequate funding for manpower, training, equipment, execution of the plan and follow up operations upon the conclusion of hostilities.

Rule Four:

Now that military intervention is imminent, contact with our allies is initiated and a coalition of forces is formed if required. Extreme caution must be exercised to avoid unintended intelligence becoming public knowledge and the opposing force learning of your intentions or timing of operations.

Rule Five:

Military leaders are given their orders, and objectives, which must result in absolutely nothing less than total victory and the unconditional surrender of the opposing force. Any considerations or conditions other than humanitarian, demanded by an enemy force will gain you nothing and only serve the opposing forces situation. They must be rejected.

<u>Rule Six</u>:
The government and the military make all preparations without revealing or "telegraphing" any dates, places or plans to the public. That's like making a TV news broadcast to the opposing force as to what, when, where and how we intend to attack. It's what stupid news reporters think we should do. However that's absolutely insane unless you're trying to promulgate disinformation and then it would work in your favor, because all the liberal networks can't get a story correct anyway.

<u>Rule Seven</u>:
When ordered our military forces engage with full force, inflicting total destruction on hostile forces. Certain locations like hospitals, schools, churches, or historic buildings, are not intentionally targeted unless they're being utilized by enemy forces for military operations and it would be a strategic advantage to do so.

<u>Rule Eight</u>:
The very nature of a military force is, train to kill and destroy, not to be referees or a police force. Make no mistake about it there will be civilian casualties, there's no way to avoid it. War is death and destruction, it's ugly, it's lethal, and it's not always precise.

<u>Rule Nine</u>:
Don't try to run the war from Washington D.C. You've given the Commanders their orders and objectives, now stay out of the way and support them. Battlefield commanders should make rules of Engagement and tactical decisions, not Washington politicians watching CNN. The commanders know more about conducting military operations than a 1st term or career politician in the White House or the U.S. Congress.

<u>Rule Ten</u>:
Finally, once the military has devastated the enemy and subdued the civilian population don't declare victory and walk away. That's the perfect time for the next dictator or unfriendly force to come in and fill the void and you'll be right back where you started. Now is the time to invest in

rebuilding THEIR country; THEIR government; THEIR infrastructure; and THEIR economy. It's a long term process, not an overnight fix. It worked in Japan, because General MacArthur understood the process and was the right man at the time.

Gen Douglas MacArthur - "It's fatal to enter any war without the will to win." "The soldier above all others prays for peace, for it's the soldier who must suffer and bear the deepest wounds and scars of war." [25]

5. <u>**Change, Good or Bad**</u>? It's a very different military than when I entered the Navy in early 1971. Some of the changes that I'm aware of are good, but I'll be right up front, I don't support a lot of the changes in our society that have now influenced the structure and make-up of military service. A fighting force is not an organization to be used for social experimentation. It's not a test tube laboratory to experiment with changes in diversity programs or to prove or disprove social experimentation of any category. Specifically, homosexuality, gender change or same sex unions.

The Vietnam War (1955-1975) was still going on when I entered the service, and it was very restrictive as to what job ratings a woman could go into. Most women were nurses assigned to naval hospitals and only a few were ever near the front lines of a combat zone. Others were in ratings such as personnel administration support or supply positions but were not allowed to accept assignment that would possibly put them in a combat situation.

The Navy did have a limited number of women get their aviator wings in the mid 1970's, but they were only allowed to fly non-combat support aircraft. It wasn't until 1978 that the Supreme Court found the ban on women in combat to be unconstitutional and later in 1979 the first female Naval aviator earns her aircraft carrier qualification. It wouldn't be until 1991 that Congress repeals the law banning women from flying in combat.

During the Persian Gulf War, many female aviators distinguished themselves flying missions in the Middle East.

At this time women are allowed to apply for just about every position in the Navy, including submarines, special warfare units and operational specialists. I personally think the military has now gone too far to the right in what women are now allowed to do, but like I said in the beginning I am an old man with old conservative ideas, values, and beliefs and that also applies to how we should treat or protect a woman. It's my opinion it won't be long before all restrictions on women will be lifted and they will have to meet the same standards as men in any assignment or specialized area if this hasn't already happened in all branches of the service.

I've already told you how stupid I think the "time out" in military boot camp is, but the most recent Supreme Court's ruling on homosexual and lesbian unions and the transgender service is the pinnacle of insanity. It's not enough that military leaders must deal with the normal family hardships of military life, but now these new circumstances are going to make running a command just that much more complicated and difficult, especially a deployable combat command. That old saying "there are no atheists in foxholes," well, guess what, there shouldn't be anyone who doesn't understand human anatomy there either!

6. **<u>Who is the enemy</u>**? Now this issue is several years old, but still relevant in today's world situation. How do you fight todays wars with the Islamic States of the Middle-East and beyond their borders? Look at all the major conflicts that America has been involved in from the Revolutionary War to the Civil War, two World Wars, Korea, and the latest Middle East Wars. In all of them there were borders, an enemy in uniforms, you knew who the enemy was and where he was located.

With the radical groups today, there are no borders that we cross to engage the enemy. They don't have the political and military structure to deal with like most sovereign states. They don't appear over the horizon all wearing army green or desert camo. These extremists can and do appear suddenly on any continent and in any country, we just don't know where or when.

In today's wars they don't come across a field in a tank, appear on the horizon with an armada of warships, or in the sky with bombers and fighter jets. Their most effective weapons are the internet, recruitment, and a lot of money. Websites that portray their "Jihad" as a just cause and promises of glory in death.

They prey on mostly the young that are searching for a purpose and direction in their lives, or they might feel like they are social outcasts looking for someone or something that will give them a purpose, a sense of belonging and security. To me they are just lost souls following a false religion and hanging onto a false hope for some reason.

Even though there are and will be sudden acts of terrorism there is not the typical warlike use of bombs and bullets in this conflict, so back to the original question, how do you fight today's war with the Islamic radicals? I don't think this is the kind of war we'll ever totally win with an unconditional surrender on the battlefield, or a cease fire treaty signed by representatives in a neutral location.

I believe our only hope is to isolate and contain their influence within the Middle East region; go after their leaders and eliminate them; disrupt their means of financing; and restrict their ability to move around from country to country. Hopefully these actions will create an atmosphere of despair within their ranks. This would be an ongoing operation for decades and I'm not sure we have the leadership in Washington that has the willingness or long term focus to sustain such an endeavor.

7. __I solemnly swear...__ As terrorist's threats around the world increase and as just about anyone in uniform or anyone wearing a badge is targeted by crazy individuals, we are constantly looking for ways of protecting ourselves and our families. Many in law enforcement will not

wear their uniforms to and from work and many of those in the military only wear their uniforms while on base. So many people are afraid of the public knowing who they are or what they do right there in their own communities.

Well, here is my take on that. I spent over 26 years in the military right along with thousands of other in uniform. We were all ready to defend every citizen's right to Life, Liberty, and the Pursuit of Happiness, not the right to be scared and have to hide in your own neighborhood, in your own home. I will not hide who I am or who I have been. I will not run or hide from bullies and domestic terrorists, but instead I will take certain precautions, and I will stand ready to defend myself and my family.

I will still fight and defend the right to LIFE, LIBERTY, and the PURSUIT OF HAPPINESS for all. Just because I am not in a military uniform anymore doesn't mean I'm released from my oath and that it doesn't apply anymore. If you see something that's not right, stop it, defend against it, report it, whatever is appropriate.

If it turns out to be nothing, then all is ok, but if it turns out to be a real threat, then you just might save someone's life. As Americans we all have an obligation to protect one another against those that would seek to destroy our communities and our way of life as free citizens in the greatest country on the planet.

8. <u>A fundamental right</u>. The 2nd Amendment to the United States Constitution, how relevant is it today? In school we learned that our revolution started because British rulers and governors were imposing unfair taxes and tariffs on the colonies without input or representation by the people to the British Crown. This became known as "No taxation without representation," and was a phrase used by Boston Minister Jonathan Mayhew during a sermon in 1750, twenty-six years before the American Revolution began.

"A well-regulated Militia, being necessary to the security of a free State, the right of the people to keep and bear Arms, shall not be infringed." [26]

Also, your homes or property could be seized by the British government without due process of law for taxes or for quartering British troops and yes, government confiscation of town armories and personal weapons, in other words....GUN CONTROL. Our founding fathers and the colonists were very aware of gun control issues and the importance of being able to protect oneself as well as the colonies thus the 2nd amendment.

The following information came from a 2012 article titled ***"The American Revolution against British Gun Control"*** by David B. Kopel, Research Director, Independence Institute, and Adjunct Professor of Advanced Constitutional Law, Denver University, Sturm College of Law.

Start: [General Gage had made every effort to disarm the colonists of Lexington, Concord, and Boston, so on July 6th, 1775, the Continental Congress adopted the ***"Declaration of Causes and Necessity of Taking Up Arms,"*** written by Thomas Jefferson and Pennsylvania lawyer John Dickinson.   One year later, July 4th, 1776, the colonies adopt the ***"Declaration of Independence."*** Included in the Declaration were the tyrannical acts of King George III that listed the king's methods for carrying out gun control in the colonies.

The British knew that without full control of the population and their weapons, they could never control America.   In 1777 Undersecretary William Knox drafted a plan entitled ***"What Is Fit to Be Done with America?"*** to ensure that there would be no future rebellions by the colonists, "the Militia Laws should be repealed, and none suffered to be re-enacted, & the Arms of all the People should be taken away, nor should any Foundry or manufacturer of Arms, Gunpowder, or Warlike Stores, be ever suffered in America, nor should any Gunpowder, Lead, Arms or Ordnance be imported into it without License...."

To the Americans of 1776 the idea that the right to keep and bear arms was only a "collective right" populous and not an "individual right" of the people would have seemed incomprehensible. Americans owned weapons individually in their homes and collectively, in their town armories and powder houses. Depending on where you lived, they were needed not only for protection, but most importantly for killing wild game for food. The colonists were not going to allow the British to confiscate their individual or their collective arms, and when they tried to do both, a Revolution began.] end [27]

Americans used their individual and their collective arms to fight against the confiscation of all arms. Americans fought and died to provide themselves a new government that would never perpetrate the tyrannical policies and abuses that had provoked the revolution. Take a good look at some other countries with one person rule and tell me if the peoples "right to bear arms" is relevant today. You bet your life, and your freedom it is!

9. **<u>Guns are not evil, people are</u>**. Staying with the subject of gun control, on January 1, 2016, Texas' new law went into effect and allows the lawful "open carry" of handguns by its citizens for the first time in over 140 years. A simple change in the Texas gun law allows a person with a handgun license issued or recognized by the State of Texas to lawfully carry a handgun of their choosing in plain view, if it's carried in a belt or shoulder holster.

Now I'm not going to argue the 2nd amendment and my right to own a weapon or the merits of the new law. I have several handguns in my home right now and I am a licensed gun owner and I've received training in both military and civilian life, but don't look for me to be walking down the street with my six-gun strapped to my side like Marshal Dillon. No, it will be concealed most of the time, but I will "open carry" at the appropriate time and gatherings.

I'm already hearing comments about how gun violence will go up and the number of murders will increase. Some people are expecting our streets to be like the old west and that all the bad guys are going to be buying and carrying guns now. Well, it's not the criminals that are going to be rushing to classes to get their handgun license and then going to buy a handgun legally. It's the law abiding citizens that want to protect themselves from criminals that will be getting their license.

The Educational Fund To Stop Gun Violence published in their 2018 report that Texas had 3,522 total deaths by guns; 114 (3%) undetermined or legal shootings; 1,145 (33%) homicides; 2,263 (64%) suicides.[28] When over half the gun deaths in the state are suicides this points more towards a mental health problem, not a gun issue.

PolitiFact an online reporting source for The Poynter Institute actually compared U.S. military deaths in Afghanistan vs. annual firearm deaths in Texas. For the year 2017 Texas firearm deaths were 3,513 compared to Afghanistan firearm deaths of 15.[29] To me they just proved that the more law abiding citizens there are trained with firearms the fewer problems you will have from those that would intend harm. The comparison was stupid anyway.

Right now, there are 45 states, including Texas that permit the open carry of firearms. What I expect to see an increase in, is unintentional discharges and people shooting themselves in the foot or forgetting the restrictions in the law and walking into places where open carry is not allowed. I don't foresee people facing off at high noon for an old fashion gunfight, but instead some criminals may get a few more surprises from individuals legally carrying a handgun.

Now let's fast forward to 2021 and the current administration's attack on the 2nd Amendment. President Biden stated on April 8, 2021 "No amendment, no amendment to the Constitution is absolute," Is he out of his mind, is he saying that our Constitution is not our lawful guiding document? What he is saying is that he has every intention of violating his oath of office.

Why is it that no one seems to understand the last four words of the amendment, "shall not be infringed." "Shall not" this means no, cannot, no way, not allowed! "Infringed" or infringement means a violation, a breach, or an unauthorized act.

To me the founders knew better than to leave certain issues or rights in the hands of a centralized government thus the Bill of Rights. The current administration wants all kinds of new federal gun control laws that include a national gun registry. This and some other laws they want would, when pasted, immediately make hundreds of thousands of lawful gun owners criminals under the new law.

There is even one provision that declares during a home invasion the home owner has a duty to "retreat" rather than confront the criminal that is breaking into your home. If you protect or defend your property, your life or the lives of your family with lethal force, you are now the criminal and will be subject to prosecution under the new law. This is one of the dumbest laws I've ever heard of, but the radical liberals and the current administration want it to pass.

Finally, in my opinion the administration of any gun laws as in registration of handguns and rifles, licenses, fees and all other aspects of ownership and right to carrier is not the federal government, but "states' rights."

10. **<u>A hero's sacrifice</u>**. One day during the Obama presidency I watched him (on TV) posthumously award the Medal of Honor to two soldiers who fought and died in France during WWI. A current representative from the unit of one recipient received the award and a daughter of the other recipient received the other soldier's award. I listened to the official read the citations describing their actions under fire. The words reminded me that military heroes' more often than not give the full measure of sacrifice for others and that their lives should never be forgotten as these men's actions almost were.

As I watched and listened to how they died under fire I cried for their memory and for the freedoms I now enjoy because of the courage and sacrifices of heroes such as these. I cried for the parents that would never see their son again. Then I remembered another hero who died for me so that I could have freedom, freedom from sin. He willingly sacrificed his life and forgave those that took it in such a cruel and dramatic way, the Roman cross. Jesus Christ, God's only Son.

11. <u>**Honor those that gave all**</u>. We all know that as Jesus was preparing his disciples for his arrest and death on the cross he told them to love one another as he had loved them. In ***John 15:13 he told them "Greater love hath no man than this, that a man lay down his life for his friends."*** This passage is often used when remembering our fallen heroes on Memorial Day and many other somber occasions.

What is the meaning of Memorial Day to us? A BBQ in the backyard or at the park with family and friends; A weekend at the lake; just a day of rest or just another workday. We have all types of activities and ceremonies around the country, but let's look at the history of this day and what it should really be about.

Many believe that Memorial Day has its roots in the Revolutionary War and in certain parts of America that could be true, but it wasn't until the late 1860's that Americans began holding springtime tributes to our fallen heroes. Following the Civil War there was the establishment of the country's first national cemeteries. Americans had begun honoring fallen soldiers by decorating their graves with flowers and reciting prayers.

It's not known exactly where the tradition first began, but in 1966, Waterloo, New York, was declared the official birthplace of Memorial Day. Waterloo which had first celebrated it 100 years before on May 5, 1866 was chosen because it hosted an annual community event during which businesses closed and residents decorated soldiers' graves with flowers and flags.

"In 1868, Commander in Chief John A. Logan of the Grand Army of the Republic issued General Order Number 11 designating May 30 as a memorial day "for the purpose of strewing with flowers or otherwise decorating the graves of comrades who died in defense of their country during the late rebellion, and whose bodies now lie in almost every city, village, and hamlet churchyard in the land."[30] The day was first known as "Decoration Day" and May 30th was chosen by General Logan because it wasn't the anniversary date of any significant battle victory or loss on record for either side.

On the first Decoration Day many northern states held commemorative events and by 1890 many states had made Decoration Day an official state holiday. Many Southern states, on the other hand, continued to honor their dead on separate days until after World War I.

Gradually the day became known as Memorial Day, but only honored those lost during the Civil War. Following WWI, it evolved to include all military personnel who died during all U.S. conflicts. The date remained May 30th until 1968 when Congress passed the "Uniform Monday Holiday Act," that established Memorial Day as a federal holiday on the last Monday in May. The law went into effect in 1971.

Old records are questionable as to the number of battlefield and other casualties, and even today there are organizations that track the numbers and are continually researching and revising their totals. The U.S. Civil War remains America's costliest war ever, with the revised numbers approaching 660,000 souls lost from both sides. It is estimated that from 1776 to 2019 the number of U.S. combat related deaths has reached 1.4 million.

Has the cost of our freedoms been too high? I don't think I can adequately answer that question, because I have no real idea what life is like without the freedoms and liberty that I have enjoyed all my life. I have a certain fear of our government to be sure, but nothing like the people that have lived under a cruel and oppressive one like Russia, China, old East Germany or of course the German government lead by Adolph Hitler during WWII.

I have no idea what it's like fearing that the police or military will come into my home and arrest me because they believe I said something bad about the government. I have no idea what it's like to be held in jail without knowing the charges or without a fair trial for months or even years. I have no idea what it's like to be held in a concentration camp.

So, what does Memorial Day mean to you and to me? It means that I'm eternally grateful to every man and woman that has served this nation so I don't have to fear our government like those I just described. I owe a debt that I will never be able to repay to those who have given their very lives for the preservation of freedom in this country and to others around the globe.

It means that all of us have an obligation to remember their sacrifices and to endeavor with all our resources, strengths, and our service, to continue to protect and defend the liberties and freedoms we hold so dear. It means to me that those that gave the "full measure" of service demand no less of me to preserve, protect and defend the freedoms that were given to us by the blood and sacrifices of those we honor on Memorial Day. This day is about courage, honor, sacrifice, and remembrance of all those that gave the "full measure" of devotion.

God bless America, those who serve this great Republic and all those who have given so much, let us all be forever grateful.

SECTION SIX
SOCIAL EQUALITY IN AMERICA

This was a rather hard section for me to write, because it involves several subjects that have been argued and debated for decades. As you will soon discover my personal opinions don't line up with many others, and don't fit in the so called politically correct category.

1. <u>**Are we all equal**</u>? First let's ask the question, is there true equality in America, after all isn't that one of the basic tenets of our own constitution?

"We hold these truths to be self-evident, that all men are created equal…" [31]

So, has GOD created all men (mankind) equally as far as our individual rights? Are all individuals treated equally and afforded the same opportunities in America? Do we as a nation and as individuals still claim this to be true? When you speak of equal rights the subject includes several different conditions that must be considered. Race, gender, disabilities, employment, religion, sex, and we could list many more if we thought about it.

Throughout American history there have come moments that question and demanded we look at our rights. With the birth of our nation, we demanded self-rule and equal representation. We created a system of laws and courts so that we would all be treated equally and have equal access to the courts irrespective of our station in life. Did an African slave, an American Indian, anyone from an Asian nation have equal access to these same laws and courts in the late 1700's, 1800's, and into the 1900's, you know they didn't. Could a woman exercise the same rights as a man when it came to the workplace, politics and voting, of course not.

It took a civil war to end slavery, the 19th amendment to the constitution in 1920 to give women the right to vote and the Civil Rights

Act of 1964 to give everyone equal rights under the law. It banned discriminatory practices in employment and ended segregation in public places such as theaters, restaurants, swimming pools, libraries, and public schools. However, even

after all our changes there is still racism and discrimination in America today and it's not all against our black citizens as the civil rights activists would have you believe.

Can we truly say that women have finally achieved equality in all areas of American society? I'm not sure if women have broken through that glass ceiling yet when it comes to equality in the workplace. There are many that would say we have gone too far past center and now we have "reverse discrimination" in many areas of the business world and employment opportunities. I for one believe this to be true in many areas of the business world.

In today's world, there are a host of new issues that must be examined and decided; do we as a nation owe equal treatment for anything and to everyone? Examples, do we have to treat homosexual unions the same as any other marriage? This year (2015) the Supreme Court said yes. Also, are you free to make up your own religion and receive the same treatment under state and federal law as all other established churches?

Do we owe immigration and citizenship as a right to anyone who comes to our shores and applies? The liberals in our government are implying all you must do is just get here. As a matter of fact the current administration is basically doing away with the borders and telling everyone come on in, you don't have to become a citizen because we'll give you whatever you need. Where do you draw the line between equality and absurdity, between rights and privileges, and between truth and the pursuit of sinful behavior?

Well, as you can very easily tell I'm no scholar on this issue, but I believe there are still a lot of unanswered questions on this topic, a lot of paths that have not yet been taken and a lot of progress that is still left to be made. I know that 100% equality is not attainable, but it's a laudable goal to strive for. I pray that GOD will show us all the way to greater equality here on earth and that it will be achieved in a much calmer manner than some of the issues of the past.

2. <u>Celebrate YOUR heritage</u>. I remember one time in Meridian, MS. I was supposed to go to a luncheon on base for Black history or Asian Pacific Islander month, I don't remember which it was, but I was tired of going to all those things. I had a lot of work to do, and I was frustrated with these "social events." I told my commander "why don't we just pick a month and whatever you are, celebrate it, and then we'll all work the other eleven months of the year."

I know this may have sounded insensitive or just lazy on my part and not wanting to participate, but that was not my intent. I don't believe that immigrants should come to America and loose or forget their customs and heritage just for the sake of "fitting in," but instead should assimilate into the great American culture, the "fabric" of our society with the rich customs and traditions of their heritage.

I believe it's wrong however for immigrants to come here and want to be considered equal, but separate and not participate wholly in the American experience. To come here and expect that this society and conditions in this country should or must change to accommodate their beliefs is completely wrong and displays a very selfish and inappropriate attitude.

There are places in Europe like London and Paris where immigrants have set up their own communities within the city and established their own laws and leaders. City officials have turned a blind eye and allowed this to happen not wanting to appear intolerant to the immigrant's culture and beliefs and in some cases police will not even patrol in those communities out of fear for their own safety.

Now this may sound bad, but does our own Indian Reservations sound a little like the same thing, except for the fact, they're not the immigrants, we are. There are dozens of "Indian Nations" throughout the U.S. and our government allows them to establish their own ruling governments, court systems and in some cases their own tribal laws. Don't we have something that says, "One Nation Under God, Indivisible, With Liberty and Justice For All." No we're not, we are a collection of many nations inside our common borders.

Now what's my purpose in this entry, what am I trying to express? Well, I guess it would be, don't lose sight of your history, your heritage, your customs, and traditions passed down by your ancestors. But remember they're yours, not mine, so celebrate, share, but don't expect the world or your local community to change or conform just for you and your ancestors.

3. <u>Affirmative Action, for who</u>? I don't know, nor have I ever believed in quotas or affirmative action programs as they were developed and implemented back in the 1960's and 1970's. They may have had good intentions, but often, I saw them used to give jobs or positions to individuals who were lesser qualified or had not yet attained the proper education, skills or training for a particular job or position. There was a time when I was participating in the job interview process that we had to select a minority regardless of qualifications.

These programs were based solely on an individual's ethnic class or gender and unfairly selected one individual over another. These selections also made it possible for an organization to show that they were following whatever ethnic/gender percentage guidelines that were currently acceptable by the federal or state government and outside activist groups. And not surprisingly no one was ever satisfied with the results. It always had to be better in some category in someone's mind.

When I was a department chief, every year I had to fill out the manpower form that broke down the rank/rating, ethnic class, and gender of all my sailors and civilian personnel and it was submitted to the manpower nerds in Washington D.C. It only showed the policy wonks in the Pentagon what ethnic group they needed to recruit more of in order to meet the current government statically percentages and served no military operational or combat readiness purpose.

As a former military leader I guarantee you that when we were getting ready for a Middle East deployment I never thought or even cared what the ethnic background of my crew was. My only concern was, are they qualified and ready to do the job we were assigned to do.

When it comes time to face an enemy in battle the color of a person's skin, what their family heritage is or do they meet current diversity standards is not even a fleeting thought in anyone's mind. The military is not a social laboratory, and such programs have no place in our armed forces. The only thing that needs to be insured is the fair and equal treatment of all personal under the guidelines of the Uniform Code of Military Justice and other military personal codes and regulations.

In today's business world, the program is called "Diversity" and does basically the same thing. Human Resource professionals will tell you that diversity involves how people perceive themselves in race, gender, ethnic group, age, personality, cognitive style, tenure, organizational function, education, background and more.

One of the main ideas is to have a workforce that mirrors the local population's demographics. Again, the deciding factor is ethnic or what race you consider yourself to be, or your gender and nothing to do with bringing the most qualifications, training, and experience to the position over all other candidates.

You would think by now we would have become a society that could look at a resume or job application and what an individual brings to the job without ever asking or seeing in writing what he or she considers as their race. We have not yet seen Dr. King's dream become reality, that his children would "one day live in a nation where they will not be judged by the color of their skin, but by the content of their character." [32] And we never will achieve that goal or real equality, as long as we have programs that are clearly based on just that, the color of your skin, your ethnic heritage or your gender. To me the programs in and of themselves are clearly a tool of discrimination against all races and both genders.

4. **Is racism always one sided**? Racism, what exactly is it? The following is from the Anti-Defamation League, it is defined as: "Racism: The marginalization and/or oppression of people of color based on a socially constructed racial hierarchy that privileges white people." [33]

Throughout my lifetime racism in America has been almost solely focused on the black race and their treatment in jobs, housing, education, and public services, but racist treatment has not been exclusive to them. Look at our own history and how we have treated the Native American Indians in the early days of our country, then later how we discriminated against each other as immigrants coming over from such places as Ireland or Scotland. How about how people of Asian descent and how they have been treated through time not just in America, but around the world.

During WWII, we confiscated almost everything that Asian citizens owned and put entire families in concentration camps here in America for no other reasons except fear and prejudice. Onboard the U.S.S. Constellation I even served with a Navy Commander of Japanese descent that was in one of those camps as an infant. Later as a Navy A-6 pilot he was shot down over North Vietnam and was held as a POW in "Hanoi Hilton" prison camp. Some say that he and other Asians that were POW's received treatment much more brutal than that received by other prisoners.

Study world history and how different races have been treated. The Jewish nation has been the recipient of some of the worst racism, and slavery thought out history from the days of bondage in Egypt to the persecution that continues today by all their neighbors. During the height of the Roman Empire look at how they treated everyone they conquered or that wasn't a Roman citizen.

In all of Africa, Central and South America and even in North America you can study the different tribes or civilizations of people and how they have treated each other as inferior races and have enslaved each other in their own regions. How about one of history's biggest example of racism and insanity, Adolph Hitler, and the German military during World War II, that was racism at its worst and over six million Jews could testify if they hadn't been mass murdered in the streets and in concentration camps.

Is there still racism in America, of course there is, and it's not aimed or centered around any one group or race of people. I have heard some people say that blacks are not capable of racism, which strikes me as one of the stupidest things I've heard on this subject. To me anytime there is discrimination against an individual or group based solely on their culturally background, skin color (black or white), gender or social status you have racism, and everyone is guilty of it at some point in their lives.

There will always be those that believe certain nationalities or groups of individuals are inferior to themselves and I believe this is the foundation on which racism is built. The principles or characteristics of racism knows no individual race, skin color, gender, or geographical location. No matter how hard we try to guard against it, racism is still with us and can be found just about anywhere, anytime.

The WEBSTER definition for racist: rac·ist / rāsəst /
noun: "Any person who demonstrates, by actions, ideas or speech to justify discrimination or prejudice against people of other races, or who believes that a particular race is superior to another."

The new liberal definition for racist:

(a) Any person, group or organization who declares or proclaims differing views or disagreement with any minority or self-proclaimed disenfranchised individual or group of individuals from any other walk of life regardless of the issue.

(b) Any person, group or organization with political views and goals that differ from those proclaimed as truth by the liberal socialist democrat party, any differing personal beliefs in religion, family and worldwide issues.

By using (a) or (b) that person is therefore by default a racist. In today's "American" society more often than not it is the racist themselves that are first to cry racism. It would seem that most of us have gotten beyond it, but some groups still need racism to prop up or justify their radical views, ideas or ill-conceived political agenda.

5. <u>This one tops the stupid scale</u>. Here's a subject that from time to time comes back up when certain events occur within the black community, "Reparations for slavery." This is the idea that some form of compensatory payment should be made to the descendants of Africans who had been enslaved as part of the Atlantic Slave Trade. The first question I must ask is, what if anything do I have to do with the acts of anyone in the past?

"A series of events in 2020 have fueled demands that Congress take steps to address racism, including the death of George Floyd, the COVID-19 pandemic and the death of Breonna Taylor, a black American woman who was shot in her home while Louisville police executed a search warrant.

In June, Robert Johnson, who became America's first Black American billionaire when he sold BET to Viacom, called for $14 trillion in reparations based on $357,000 for each 40 million African Americans."[34]

Do I have a responsibility for what happened to past generations? How about what was done to the Japanese-Americans during WWII or the Chinese slave labor of the early 1800's. How far back in history do you go? Am I responsible for what the Vikings or the early Romans did if I have a blood line that goes back to them? How do all blacks prove they are direct descendants of someone that was held in slavery? There were free blacks back then.

To me, all this is just the efforts of a small percentage of people that want another "entitlement." What can I get for free? The only things that this generation or any generation to come owes to the black community is to see that it never happens again here or anywhere else we can. We have a moral responsibility to ensure that everyone is treated fairly and equally under the law.

This idea of reparations could be applied to so many different occurrences from past world history, but where do you stop. You stop it here and now; we don't owe any amount of money or property to anyone for the sins of past generations. Just because someone steps up and says my great, great, great grandfather was a slave on a Mississippi plantation and he was never paid for his labor, is no justification for me or any other tax payer to make "reparations" ever. THE END.

6. <u>Sexual Immorality</u>. Reluctantly I'm going to give this subject of immoral behavior it's 15 minutes, but before I do let me say that all the excuses these people come up with are a bunch of damnable lies. "I didn't have a choice, GOD made me this way." "I feel I was meant to be a woman." "I can't help having these feelings, that's just the way I was made." For decades' proponents of equal rights for the homosexuals, lesbians and the transgender movement have been spewing their lies on the streets of America, in the media around the world and in our court systems.

The only thing I'm going to say about the transgender crowd is that Satan has absolutely gotten into this person's head. The reasons and excuses for doing this are lies straight from the pits of HELL. Your body (gender) and your spirit (human soul) are what God made you and nothing you do in this world will change that. There is NO reason, NO justification, neither mentally or physically for anyone to do it or have it done.

Sadly, on June 26, 2015 the Supreme Court ruled in a 5 to 4 decision that same sex civil unions are Constitutional. I won't argue with the Supreme Court on the Constitution, we'll leave that for another day, but I will argue that these unions, as they are called, are all Biblically and humanly unnatural and very wrong! There is NO debate or conversation needed on this subject for me.

The GOD who created this universe and all things in it; the GOD that made us, MALE and FEMALE, has already given us the answer to this issue and that makes it final. The union of two people of the same sex is unnatural. It's against the natural order of creation and the laws of GOD. It's perverse morally wrong. Am I being too blunt, am I too insensitive on the subject? Yes, I am! But just maybe it's about time more Christians stand up and speak out about what is in GOD's Word and what we know to be the truth in our hearts and in His Word.

They like to call themselves Gay, but when I was growing up that was someone's name? Also, that's the name on the side of the famous WWII aircraft that dropped the first atomic bomb, the Enola Gay? It's a word used to express a human emotion. I have and always will call them by their proper name, HOMOSEXUALS, LESBIAN, and all acts of sexual immorality is a perversion condemned by GOD.

Romans 1:26-27: 26. "That's why GOD abandoned them to degrading lust. Their females traded natural sexual relations for unnatural sexual relations. 27. Also, in the same way, the males traded natural sexual relations with females, and burned with lust for each other. Males performed shameful actions with males, and they were paid

back with the penalty they deserved for their mistake in their own bodies." [35]

I haven't conducted any long studies on the subject; I'm not a Preacher or a Biblical scholar, and I don't need to be. I'm a sinner saved by GOD's grace. Furthermore, there is no one on this planet that can make me believe that the GOD who created this universe, the GOD that made each one of us in His image ever made a mistake in His creation.

GOD DOES NOT MAKE MISTAKES!!!

There is no issue of equal rights with these people. They don't deserve any more or any less rights and privileges than anyone else, unless you want to classify their actions as a mental illness. There are many other references throughout the Bible to show us that GOD's intent was only one union, Male and Female and that anything else is an abomination in His sight. GOD's Word is the final word on this subject.

7. **<u>Legalized Murder</u>**. I'm not sure if this is the right section to talk about abortion, but here goes. In no way can I address the subject from a woman's perspective, so I won't try. I realize this is a huge "hot button" issue for a lot of people and has been one of the biggest political issues of our time, but I can only support one view, LIFE.

I don't believe that God's word condones abortion, and I don't believe our Constitution guarantees a woman the right to have one, if anything they both support life. This issue has nothing to do with women's equality or personal rights over their own body's as many proponents have tried to argue. It does however have everything to do with the sanctity of a human life created by a righteous and loving GOD.

My personal belief is that life begins at conception, when the very first cell is formed, I believe that is the beginning of a human life. Before that first human cell there was nothing, but when that first cell forms in a woman's womb that is LIFE. God created, God given LIFE. If that child is not to be born, not to survive, it's not up to any earthly power or government policy, politician, or abortion activist, only GOD has that power. God, and God alone has the knowledge and the power to make that decision.

Some will now ask what about in the case of incest, rape or when the life of the mother is in jeopardy? Must a mother suffer the pain and indignity of a child as a result of such violent and horrifying event. Shall a mother be required to forfeit her life for that of an unborn child. How do we answer these questions?

Again, I'm not without compassion for the woman, but I must be on the side of all human life. I will not sit in judgement over a woman and her decision in such cases. I don't have the right to, that is between her and GOD. Only GOD knows what should be done and only a Holy GOD will sit in perfect judgement over all of us. I would hope that the woman would pray and seek GOD's will no matter what the circumstances are.

Well, what do you think God is going to do, yell in her face or whisper in her ear what she should do? It just might be that simple or there could be many other things to occur that gives God's direction to her.

I'm not smart enough to argue if it is or is not murder as if we were in a court of law, but abortion on demand simply for convenience however is nothing short of a criminal act in my opinion and there should be laws and strong punishments in our society against it.

The organization Planned Parenthood has been in the news over the past few years about the funding they receive and the services they provided to women, specifically abortion counseling, services, and the selling of human fetuses. I will simply say that any organization that participates in abortion should not receive any federal or state taxpayer dollars and should be publicly discredited or even prosecuted for their abortion practices.

In respect to equality on this subject I would simply say equal access to women's counseling and health care yes, equal access to abortion services on demand, MURDER.

Deuteronomy 30:19 "I call heaven and earth to record this day against you, that I have set before you, life and death, blessing and cursing: therefore, choose life, that both thou and thy seed may live." [36]

8.   **TOTAL ABSURDITY**.   The following list is believed to come from Ted Nugent as he shares his reflections on why, as he puts it, "we are living in an upside-down world". In my view this is the America we live in today.

• If a man pretends to be a woman, you're required to pretend with him.

• Russians influencing our elections are bad, but illegal aliens voting in our elections are good.

• Citizens are fined if they don't buy their own health insurance, and then they are forced to buy it for illegals.

• People who have never owned slaves should pay slavery reparations to people who have never been slaves.

• Irish doctors and German engineers who want to immigrate must go through a rigorous vetting process, but any illiterate Central American gang-banger who jumps the southern fence is welcome.

• $5 billion for border security is too expensive, but $1.5 trillion for "free" health care for illegals is not.

• If you cheat to get into college you go to prison, if you cheat to get into the country you go to college for free.

• Politicians who say the President is not above the law, put illegal immigrants and themselves above the law.

• People who say there is no such thing as gender are the same ones demanding a female President.

• Illegals don't pay taxes, but they get tax refunds.

• We see other countries going Socialist and collapsing, and it seems like a great plan to us!

• Some people are held responsible for things that happened before they were born, and other people are not held responsible for what they are doing right now.

• Criminals are catch-and-released to hurt more people but stopping them is somehow bad because it's a violation of THEIR rights.

• And pointing out all this hypocrisy somehow makes you politically incorrect, uninformed or a "racists."

SECTION SEVEN
POLITICS AND THE WORLD

This is another section containing several of today's hot button issues about the current government, elections and about many of today's issues around the world.

"I am concerned for the security of our great Nation; not so much because of any threat from without, but because of the insidious forces working from within." Douglas MacArthur [37]

In many circles, it's considered bad manners to publicly discuss one's finances, politics or religion. I really don't like talking about "religions," but I will be glad to tell you the "Good News" about the gift of Salvation and our Savior Jesus Christ. Well, it's easy to see that I'm breaking this tradition and talking about all of the above in this little book and in this section, it's politics!

1. **Will they compromise**? After just about any national election the party that is now the minority always asks the question of the majority party "will they compromise; will they reach across the aisle in the spirit of cooperation?" And the guiltiest of this agenda is the media.

Well, that's one of the most stupid ideas I've heard in today's American politics and not what I voted for. My vote is never for compromise, my vote is not for cooperating with the Democrats when the Republicans have the majority. I'm not voting for and sending representatives to Washington or to the state capital to compromise on my values and what I believe needs to be done for our country.

My vote was for Representatives to act like they are in charge and do what they know to be right for the country and the people they are supposed to be representing. They need to conduct the business of "We The People" without regard to party agendas or who is in a position to dictate or make demands on any legislation of the bills being considered.

2. <u>Check Your Religion At The Door</u>. Why do so many Americans believe that Politics and Religion shouldn't mix? In those words I just might agree. I don't want any politician coming into our houses of worship dictating how we should conduct our service, what we should believe or interjecting government policies. Conversely I don't want our Christian leaders in the halls of congress dictating to our elected officials how the government should be run according to the many different Biblical views.

However, that does not mean that our elected officials need to check their faith or their Christian principles at the door when they assemble. God has given us instruction on how we are to conduct ourselves in our daily lives, at home, in our jobs, in our relationships with one another. If I'm being presented some issue, piece of legislation, a process or any other condition that must be decided upon I will reject if it is unethicle, morally wrong or in direct conflict with my faith and belief in the Bible.

We've seen the purging of God's word, our faith and beliefs out of our lives for decades now. Public prayer has been forbidden in so many venues like our schools or sporting events. People use to attend public prayer events on a National Day of Prayer in churches, our workplaces, social organizations and yes, even in the halls of congress. Today I think they're still around, but you never here them widely promoted or attended as we once saw. People have demanded that the Ten Commandments or any other Christian symbols be taken down from any government building.

The great evangalistist Billy Graham wrote about two reasons why Religion and Politics cannot be separated. "First, we human beings are deeply and inescapably religious, and religion cannot be defined restrictively as the worship of a supernatural deity." He goes on to say that not everyone worships the God of the Bible, but they worship someone of something that "might be sex, money, power, or success. But it is a god and a functional savior nonetheless. Often, it is the combination of two or more objects of worship. In other words, the human heart is a playground for the gods."

"Second, we cannot separate our private self from our public self.…As the Bible defines it, religion is the central organizer of a person's thoughts and loves. If a person really and truly embraces the God of Jesus as the Creator and Lord of the universe, that embrace will have a cascade effect, pouring down and out into that person's beliefs, feelings, values, and actions." [38]

However weak or strong the majority of the founding fathers of our nation held with Christian beliefs and the power of a higher being. You can see it in their writings and the documents about them. They knew and understood the importance of their faith in their everyday lives and in the leadership of the nation they were building. We need men and women of strong Christain faith in leadership positions today. We need Christian integraty and people with strong morale standards leading us in all government positions.

3. **A Political Scourge**! Political Correctness (PC): "Someone who is politically correct believes that language and actions that could be offensive to others, especially those relating to sex and race, should be avoided. A politically correct word or expression is used instead of another one to avoid being offensive. Avoiding language or behavior that any particular group of people might feel is unkind or offensive."[39] The term was first coined sometime back in the early 1970's. Now today PC has invaded just about every aspect of our daily lives, impacting us in our jobs, our social life and even in our homes.

It's the incremental process of controlling free speech and what we should or should not think. It tells us what we should think about a specific subject, words that we can no longer use because some group has given them a different meaning and they could possibly be offensive to someone of a different race, a different culture or those who are "more progressive" in their attitudes and beliefs. Political Correctness is a valuable tool used by those with a specific agenda or those in government and academia to control different areas of our lives, social programs, and political and educational information.

Let's look at some words that have changed over time. We used to say spokesman, but now it's spokesperson. It used to be Congressman or Congresswoman, but now it's simply Representative. We always called them Fireman and Policeman, but you can't do that now. It must be Firefighter and Police Officer. We used to have a Chairman or chairwoman, but now it must be a Chair or Chairperson. There are no more Mailman or Mailmen, they are now called Mail Carrier or Letter Carrier.

The next time you go to a restaurant and the young man or woman comes up to your table and introduces themselves to you, listen to what they say. "Hi, my name is Mary, and I will be your waitress." No, it will be either "Hi, my name is Mary, and I will be your server, or I will be taking care of you." All titles must be gender neutral.

Now here are some examples of PC out of control:

a) State workers were told by management that they should not use the words "citizen" and "brown bag" because they could potentially be offensive to illegals in the community.

b) A university professor was banned from even mentioning the concept of intelligent design because it would supposedly "violate the academic integrity" of the course that he was teaching.

c) A university student was ordered to take off a cross that she was wearing because someone not of the same faith "could be offended."

d) A high school track team was disqualified because one of the runners "made a gesture thanking GOD" once he crossed the finish line.

e) A teacher in New Jersey was fired for giving his own Bible to a student that didn't own one.

f) I just read several articles about the writing of the Constitution and the Bill of Rights by the men who formed our country and our government.

They were no longer referred to as the "founding fathers," but instead called the "founding generation," gender neutral.

g) One that is very popular right now, changing the names of sports teams or their team logos. Examples: Atlanta Braves, Washington Redskins, or the Cleveland Indians. This is just a few of the hundreds of high school, college and pro teams that have been forced by political correctness running rampant through our country.

"Congress shall make no law respecting an establishment of religion or prohibiting the free exercise thereof; or abridging the freedom of speech, or of the press; or the right of the people peaceably to assemble, and to petition the Government for a redress of grievances." [40]

4. <u>**You Can't Say That**</u>. Continuing with the subject of speech let's look next at the first amendment to the Constitution. Considering it's the first tells me how important this subject was to our founding fathers. In this entry, I am addressing the freedom of speech and how this freedom and the first amendment is under constant attack by socialist liberals and the uninformed fools in our society today.

Recently there have been many stories in the media about what is freedom of speech, what words or phrases are acceptable. The faculty and students on many college campuses are claiming that the first amendment is "out of date," that a person can't just say anything they want, so there must be limitations on our speech. It's a very one sided issue with most liberals; I can say whatever I want if it helps or furthers my liberal views or objectives. You on the other hand can't use certain words or phrases if in my mind, they are in any way critical or offensive to me, real or imagined.

I will admit this is a hard one, how far can someone go in their speech; are your personal actions, your physical expressions also covered under this amendment; where do you draw the line, or do you? Who has the authority to regulate what words we use and in what manner we use them?

There must be limits in order to have a civil and orderly society. I think you can say whatever you want to on any subject, just know that all speech has consequences. You can't verbally threaten someone with bodily harm or death just because you want to. You can't publicly say things that could cause a dangerous condition such as yelling fire in a crowded public building when there is no fire.

Now what about your physical actions, are they considered a matter of "free speech?" Well, if you want to go walking down the sidewalk without any cloths on, NO. If you want to hold up a sign against the police and go walking down the middle of a busy street, NO. There are other things that some will call their right of "free expression" such as night club activities, pornography, the way they dress or look. This may be true, but society must place restrictions on such activities in order to protect our children or to maintain safety and order in our communities.

When our founding fathers wrote the Constitution and the Bill of Rights and considered what is "free speech," I'm sure they didn't have a crystal ball to look into the future to see how we would be defining what it was. In fact, I've read that there were several disagreements about what to write and that they chose their words very carefully.

In their day, the main issue was the British Crown. Their purpose was to ensure in the new country they were forming, there would be no king or queen at the head of the government. And with that, the people would have the right to freely express themselves, including their disagreement with their government and the people that ran it without fear of reprisal. Thus, the first amendment guaranteeing that the government would make no law abridging (curtailing or restricting) their right to freely express their opinions in a private or public forum.

I'm not sure if I've adequately expressed my thoughts and opinions on this subject, but I hope you will clearly understand. I know that just like the second amendment, the right to keep and bear arms, the first amendment and our freedom to express ourselves is under attack from an ever increasing liberal socialist movement in almost every part of our society. If we continue to stand by and do nothing there will come a time in our future that just talking to your friends and neighbors could have dangerous consequences.

"I do not agree with what you have to say, but I'll defend to the death your right to say it." Voltaire [41]

5. <u>Language does not control me</u>. Continuing with the subject of speech did you know that there is a publication that is considered by many in academia and some in government to be their official guide for today's proper use of language? The following comments are from the opening statement in the introduction of the "Bias Free Language Guide" that was published on the University of New Hampshire website in 2013. After a huge uproar UNH removed it from their website in 2015. The City of Dubuque, Iowa however has posted the entire guide in their document center on their website as a part of their "Intercultural Competency Initiative" for employees.

"Language as Leadership: Language has been described as complicated, intriguing and beautiful. Benjamin Lee Whorf said, "Language shapes the way we think, and determines what we can think about." Some writers have commented on language as the biggest barrier to human progress because, as Edward de Bono said, "Language is an encyclopedia of ignorance. Old perceptions are frozen into language and force us to look at the world in an old-fashioned way."

All things considered, individuals are both beneficiaries and victims of whatever language traditions they are born into. Universities are places to look at the world in new ways. As a university organization, we care about the life of the mind. We offer this guide as a way to promote discussion and to facilitate creative and accurate expression." [42]

Well, like it or not here are my opinions on this subject. There is no question, languages are sometimes very complicated, but our ability to effectively express ourselves knows no limitations. Language does not shape or determine what I think but provides me the conduit in which I use to communicate to you, my ideas, my beliefs, or desires just as I am doing in this book right now.

What I think about and the way I think is not determined by my language, but by the events that continuously occur around me. Ignorance is shown only by those who fail to study and practice the use of their language. Words in any language are most often derived in part or whole from a word with a specific meaning in another language. Thus, the part of the reason I always say that words have meaning.

My "old fashioned ways" are not a result of the language I learned as a child, but instead a result of the values, traditions, and teachings I received from my parents and other caring adults. I am not a victim of time or language, but I am made richer by the knowledge of both and the ability to clearly express my thoughts and opinions. Just because some university professor or group with an agenda decides to change the meaning of a word or the manner in which a specific word can be used does not make it accurate and certainly does not create a new truth that the rest of mankind must conform too.

The reason I started writing this entry is because I saw an article that lead me to the University of New Hampshire website where I found the guide. It really raised my blood pressure to read in the language guide don't use the word "American." It made all the morning news shows and made me mad as…. well let's just say very mad!

In their view using the word "American" is problematic, because depending on the context it fails to recognize South America. According to the guide we should call ourselves U.S. citizens or residents of the U.S. This is just dumber than dirt.

They claim that depending on the context in which, "American" is used it leaves out the people of South America. The PC speech police have absolutely lost their liberal minds on this one. I am an "American" a proud citizen of the United States of America and I make no apologies for using the word. When I use the word American it will be obvious who I am talking about. If I am talking about someone in South America, I will refer to their specific country. By the way they left out of their little book those in Central America. I will use words that leave no doubt as to who and what country I am speaking about.

This is the kind of junk in our educational system that has very little, if any, value, and our children can absolutely do without it. The guide was found on the university's website until it was removed on 7/30/2015 and according to a University of New Hampshire statement by President Mark W. Huddleston, "This 'guide' was developed by a small group of faculty and staff in 2013 and is NOT UNH policy."

Also, in that same statement UNH president Mark Huddleston said, "It's ironic that what was probably a well-meaning effort to be 'sensitive' proves offensive to many people, myself included." [43] However, as you can see the damage has already been done. Organizations are now starting to adopt it as a part of their diversity or personnel policies and training.

6. <u>Politics or Religion</u>. This one could go in either section depending on how you look at it. For the second time in a year (2015) we had a foreign leader make a speech to the Congress and the American public. First it was Israeli Prime Minister Benjamin Netanyahu and then Pope Francis who started his first ever tour of America with his first stop in Washington D.C.

He first met with Obama and the next day he became the first Pope in history to make an address to a joint session of Congress. I think this one is more politics than religion. With some difficultly he gave his speech in English with the Speaker of the House, John Boehner, in view over his left shoulder and visibly moved with emotion.

The Pope entered the chamber like it was the President's State of the Union speech. As he began his speech, that lasted just under an hour, he referred to America as the land of the free and home of the brave, how great a country America was and why people wanted to come here. It wasn't long though until he got right to the politics, making statements about immigration, abortion, and the death penalty. He should stick to the business of the church and seeking out lost souls.

7. **How it's supposed to be done**. Back in 2015 I witnessed a changing of the guard in the House of Representatives. A new Speaker of the House, Paul Ryan of Wisconsin taking over from John Boehner. There was a calm and organized vote as the role was called and each member rose and verbally cast their vote just as they have done it for over two hundred years.

The minority leader from the other party paid tribute to the outgoing speaker and introduced to the full house the new speaker with words of praise and hope. It was a moment in history that no matter what their political differences are, they all came together as one house to celebrate the process, the tradition, the Constitution, and the type of people we are.

It was a joyous occasion that made me feel proud that we are a country that can have this type of political power change without physical violence and the hatred you may see in other countries and other governments. Just a moment, fast forward to Nancy Pelosi as House Speaker. In President Trump's State of the Union, she is seen at the end of the speech standing and ripping her copy of the speech in half in front of everyone in the joint session. When she is gone I pray that we will never see the likes of someone as simple minded, undignified and vindictive as that woman again.

"A leader without anyone following is just taking a walk."

Former Rep. John Boehner [44]

With all our problems, all our arguments and disagreements I'm still convinced we have the best system of government on the planet. No matter how much I may complain, I wouldn't trade this country or our government and our laws for any others in the world.

8. <u>**The Invasion of the Illegals**</u>. Earlier I briefly mentioned illegal aliens and how out of control it is in America. Here the politically correct (PC) police have struck again. The term "illegal alien" is the correct legal term to use, however, the PC police have stated that "a person cannot be illegal." Therefore, their new title is "undocumented immigrant." Horseradish, when they're caught, they're documented and they're illegal because they have not gone through the legal immigration process. It matters not what their plight in life is, they are still "Illegal Aliens." [45]

The new democrat administration has now closed some border checkpoints and has turned the detention centers into welcome and assistance centers for the herds of "illegal aliens" coming across our southern border. Border Patrol Officers are not enforcing the law, they have become welcome agents helping "illegal aliens" get on a bus to the destination of their choice. Currently America no longer has a southern border, but an open door.

The following information is from the Migration Policy Institute, a "Think Tank" on immigration and national policies dated February 11, 2021 and you will see they use the incorrect term also for illegal aliens. They are located in Washington D. C. and in Brussels, Belgium.

<u>**How many unauthorized immigrants are in the United States**</u>: The Migration Policy Institute (MPI) has estimated there were about 11 million unauthorized immigrants in the United States in 2018. Almost half resided in three states: California (24 percent), Texas (16 percent), and New York (8 percent). The vast majority (81 percent) lived in 178 counties with 10,000 or more unauthorized immigrants each, of which the top five—Los Angeles County, CA; Harris County, TX; Dallas County, TX; Cook

County, IL; and Orange County, CA—accounted for 19 percent of all unauthorized immigrants. The top five countries of birth for unauthorized immigrants were Mexico (51 percent), El Salvador (7 percent), Guatemala (5 percent), and India and Honduras (4 percent each).

How many people are covered by Temporary Protected Status: Since 1990, 22 countries have been designated for TPS. Ten countries currently are designated: El Salvador, Haiti, Honduras, Nepal, Nicaragua, Somalia, South Sudan, Sudan, Syria, and Yemen. In 2020, an estimated 319,000 people from these ten countries had maintained active status under TPS, with the largest groups being Salvadorans (195,000), Hondurans (57,000), and Haitians (46,000).

How many apprehensions of unauthorized immigrants occur at the border annually: CBP reported 405,000 enforcement encounters at both the southern and northern borders in FY 2020. Removals and returns, which are carried out both by ICE and CBP, result in the confirmed movement of inadmissible or deportable aliens out of the United States. DHS reported a total of 531,300 removals and returns during FY 2019. CBP carried out 264,100 removals and returns in FY 2019, up 39 percent from 190,300 a year earlier. ICE carried out 267,300 removals and returns in FY 2019, a 4 percent increase from the prior year. CBP data on FY 2020 returns and removals were not available at the time of writing." [46]

On another statistical website [47] they also report all these similar numbers, but they go on to report things like the economic effect of illegal immigrants.

a.   Estimated personal income tax paid = over 1.1 billion in 2014.
b.   Estimated property tax paid = 3.6 billion in 2014.
c.   Estimated sales and excise tax paid = 7 billion in 2014.

If these people are here "illegally" then why is the employer that is taking out income tax not in jail for hiring an illegal alien?   Why is an illegal alien allowed to buy property in the very country they have entered without authorization? Other than a Consultant Card, a Temporary Resident Card or a Passport from their home country how does an illegal alien get any type of U.S. documentation such as a driver's license?

America has its whole immigration system so messed up now it's doubtful that we will ever get under control before becoming just another third world country overrun with the illegals from every other nation.

We desperately need to scrap the current system and come up with a strong immigration policy. We need a policy that secures our physical borders and effectively controls the flow and number of new immigrants coming into this country LEGALLY. Illegal immigration must be stopped as much as humanly possible and treated as a serious crime not a social condition.

9.   The Political Campaigns.   Here is where I wanted to jump headfirst into the past political campaigns and all the lies and miss information we had to suffer through. We had 8 years of tearing down and apologizing for who we are as Americans by the Obama gang.

Our image on the world stage and our trust by our allies was seriously compromised. Our military was so badly managed by the Obama administration that senior military leaders were leaving the service the service as soon as they could. They highjacked the entire healthcare industry and now the government tells doctor's and insurance companies what level of care you're entitled to. To make it worse the government controls the price of health care and levies fines when you don't purchase a policy that is sometimes triple the price you paid before Obamacare.

Depending on how the liberal historians write the history books I believe the Obama presidency will go down as one of the worst 21st century administrations in our country's history. When comparing to past Democrat presidency's it's very close to being even worse than the Carter Administration. He came in with the outlook of "hope and change" saying that his administration would be completely transparent. What we got instead was one of the most lawless and divisive administrations ever.

When he failed to get his way with Congress, he stated that he had a "phone and a pen" and he would use the power of executive orders to go around Congress and to get what he wanted. When he goes overseas, he bows to Muslim leaders and apologizes for world actions by America. All the Republicans can do is complain, hold committee meetings, pick out the color of the carpet in their office or whatever else they do.

Like many in the modern day Democrat Party the rules apply to everyone else, and you should not judge him by his actions, but by his good intentions regardless of the outcome. Then we had sadly just 4 years of rebuilding under President Trump. A lot of people didn't like him primarily because of his personality and his brashness and outspoken ways.

Well, that got to me sometimes too, but the thing about Trump is that he is not a Politian in the typical mold of someone that gets elected and then re-elected until they have been in Washington for 30 years. Trump is a businessman, and he had some very different views and ideas about how to rebuild the national interests of the country. The following information can be found on FactCheck.org posted January 20th, 2020 [48] reflecting the first three years of the Trump presidency.

a) 6.7 million jobs we added, and unemployment fell to 3.5%.

b) The economy grew at a 2.1% rate most recently.

c) Stock prices hit record high levels.

d) Poverty decreased by 0.9%, and paychecks grew 2.5% after inflation.

e) Homeownership increased by 1.1%.

The country was doing great until the onset of the Coronavirus that effected every country in the world and would have made no difference who was in office when it hit. Democrat or Republican, no one was going to pass a bill or issue an executive order and make it go away.

Now the disaster of 2020 and I don't mean the COVID-19 virus. I'm talking now about the election of Joe Biden and the first female Vice President, what's her name….never mind. Too make matters worse we now have a majority of Democrats in the House and the Senate with Nancy Pelosi, Chuck Schumer and the President of the Senate that lady, what's her name….never mind.

We really do have a three ring circus, but which one is the "Ring Master?" I think our only hope is that they screw things up so bad that the Republicans get the congress back in 2022. I don't want to see things go wrong, but the Democrats are in charge. That's a little like making public enemy #1 the mayor of the city.

10. <u>America In Decline</u>. Is our country in its declining years? Look back in history at the great civilizations and empires of the past like the Roman, the Greek, the Egyptian or the Ottoman. They all eventually fell into decline or were taken over by other civilizations. When ancient Israel turned away from God they were conquered by other countries and taken into captivity numerous times. They were liberated only after they returned to worshipping and honoring the only true God that created the Heavens and the earth.

Look at America and many other nations too at how immoral we have become as humans and the things we worship here on earth and not God. Only 24% of the American population admit to attending some form of worship in church. Why is this so bad? We live 24x7 lives with people working all types of different schedules. During our time off we want to relax, party, have fun at the beach or any number of other activities.

We don't want to be in a stuffy old church with a minister telling us we're sinners and bound for Hell if we don't repent. We all have hobbies, activities or just things that are more important to many people than taking time to worship God and a Risen Savior, and anytime those are more important, then that is the god you worship.

Lead by the Liberals and the Democrats look at the attitudes and activities we accept or encourage. Abortion, the murder of innocent life. Corruption in government from city to state house to our nation capital. The language and sexual conduct or violence of movies and TV programs. The same with the electronic games and activities we allow our children be exposed too. The immoral and damnable actions conducted by homosexuals, lesbians and transgender people that a righteous God never intended to occur.

I believe America just may have become the new region of Sodom and Gomorrah and should we not return to our faith and worship in a Heavenly God and His Holy Word we are destine for horrible times. Times of pain and suffering unlike any that today's world has ever seen.

I'm not a prophet or someone that can see into the future, so don't take my word. Read the Word of God, it's in there and He tells you what to expect. Pray for America and our people to return to the God that created us and has blessed us as a nation. **"Self-centered indulgence, pride and a lack of shame over sin are now emblems of the American lifestyle." Billy Graham** [49]

11. <u>You Could Have Heard A Pin Drop</u>. Here are several interesting stories that have to do with politics or politicians. They were found on Gabe's Fascinating Stories blog site.[50]

President John Kennedy's Secretary of State, Dean Rusk, was in France in the early 60's when Charles de Gaulle decided to pull out of NATO. de Gaulle said he wanted all U.S. military out of France as soon as possible. Rusk responded, "Does that include those who are buried here?" de Gaulle did not respond. You could have heard a pin drop.

When in England at a fairly large conference, Colin Powell was asked by the Archbishop of Canterbury if our plans for Iraq were just an example of 'empire building' by George Bush. He answered by saying, "Over the years, the United States has sent many of its fine young men and women into great peril to fight for freedom beyond our borders. The only amount of land we have ever asked for in return is enough to bury those that did not return." You could have heard a pin drop.

There was a conference in France where a number of international engineers were taking part, including French and American. During a break, one of the French engineers came back into the room saying, "Have you heard the latest dumb stunt Bush has done? He has sent an aircraft carrier to Indonesia to help the tsunami victims. What does he intend to do, bomb them?"

A Boeing engineer stood up and replied quietly, "Our carriers have three hospitals on board that can treat several hundred people; they are nuclear powered and can supply emergency electrical power to shore facilities; they have three cafeterias with the capacity to feed 5,000 people three meals a day, they can produce several thousand gallons of fresh water from sea water each day, and they carry half a dozen helicopters for use in transporting victims and injured to and from their flight deck. We have eleven such ships. How many does France have?" You Could have heard a pin drop.

A U.S. Navy admiral was attending a naval conference that included admirals from the American, English, Canadian, Australian, and French Navies at a cocktail reception. He found himself standing with a large group of officers that included personnel from most of those countries. Everyone was chatting away in English as they sipped their drinks when a French admiral suddenly complained that, whereas Europeans learn many languages, Americans learn only English.

He then asked, "Why is it that we always have to speak English in these conferences rather than speaking French?" Without hesitating, the American admiral replied, "Maybe it's because the Brit's, Canadians,

Aussie's and Americans arranged it so you wouldn't have to speak German." You could have heard a pin drop.

Robert Whiting, an elderly gentleman of 83, arrived in Paris by plane. At French customs, he took a few minutes to locate his passport in his carry on. "You have been to France before, monsieur?" the customs officer asked sarcastically. Mr. Whiting admitted that he had been to France previously. "Then you should know enough to have your passport ready."

The American said, "The last time I was here, I didn't have to show it." "Impossible, Americans always have to show their passports on arrival in France!" The American senior gave the Frenchman a long hard look. Then he quietly explained, "when I came ashore at Omaha Beach on D-Day in 1944 to help liberate this country, I couldn't find a Frenchmen to show a passport to." You could have heard a pin drop.

SECTION EIGHT
IN THE NAME OF RELIGION

This section is mostly sad. All the lies, hate and destruction being committed in the name of religion or because someone has polluted the minds of others looking for direction in their lives. Also, my thoughts on religion in America and how sometimes it's misguided for personal gain.

1. <u>Let's define Religion</u>. You would not believe how many different definitions there are of religion or being religious. I will just share this one: "Religion is a system of beliefs and practices by means of which a group of people struggle with the ultimate problem of human life." ... "Religion is that system of activities and beliefs directed toward that which is perceived to be of sacred value and transforming power." I have no idea what any of that means and a lot of others that I have read while writing this entry. I do know one thing, **RELIGION WILL SEND YOU STRAIGHT TO HELL**.

Now that's a bold statement so I guess I should explain myself. If I'm asked what religion I am I always answer that I'm a sinner saved by the grace of God and the blood of Jesus Christ. I don't tell them I attend a Southern Baptist Church unless they ask me where I go to church. And by the way the "church" is those that have accepted God's free gift of salvation, not the building we all meet in. The Baptist denomination just happens to be the one that I believe strictly teaches the Whole Word of God, the Holy Bible.

There are too many people out there that are attending houses of worship on holidays, when they feel bad about themselves or it's a part of their "social status" in their jobs and their community. They go in, set down and let a minister do all the worshiping for them, then they go through the motions of any ceremonial beliefs and then go home and feel good about themselves as if that will get them through the gates of heaven.

I don't have "religion" I have Jesus Christ as my Lord and Savior. I can't work my way into heaven or sit quietly in a pew and expect that will be sufficient. A priest or a minister can't get me into heaven and no religious beliefs or ceremonies will magically open the gates. Religion will send you straight to hell. Religion is a falsehood, a road straight to the front gates of hell. Understanding salvation is very simple to me.

John 14:6 "Jesus said to him, "I am the way, the truth, and the life. No one comes to the Father except through Me."

Romans 10:13 "For whoever calls on the name of the Lord shall be saved."

Eternity with God in Heaven is simple, believe with all your heart, with all your mind that Jesus Christ died for your sins on the cross and on the 3rd day He came forth from the grave and now sits at the right hand of the Father. Believe in Jesus, believe in God's word, accept the free gift of salvation and be saved.

1. **<u>Does the church still have a pulse</u>**? Does the church in America or even in the world still have a pulse? If you ask someone if they believe in God or a higher being most will tell you yes but ask them how often they attend church and are they actively involved in any of their church programs.   I doubt you'll get a truthful answer from most.

It's my opinion that today's Christian church is on life support and the numbers are getting worse for a number of reasons. The Statista Research Department published on January 15, 2021 there latest results on church attendance in the U.S.[51]

The way I read this data is you have between 24 to 33% that say they attend church on a weekly or almost weekly basis. The 11% that say they attend once a month are those that are members of a church, but they probably come at Easter and Christmas or when there's a wedding or funeral. More than 55% that say seldom or never attend church is because they're sleeping in or enjoying their weekend recreation activities before going back to work on Monday morning, been there, done that. The 3% that had no opinion couldn't find a church even if they drove their car through the front doors with Saint Peter standing there to greet them.

Why is church attendance so low and getting worse? I'm not a church scholar so I won't try to site all kinds of reasons, but the most recent reason is of course the Coronavirus. People are taking the precautions, some mandated by some level of government, to stay away from crowds such as church, family events, sporting events and so on. Every time you were even suspected of coming in contact with some person that had or might have been exposed to the virus you had to quarantine yourself for 7 to 14 days. You had to be tested and get a negative result before you could go just about anywhere.

I had the virus, but it wasn't as hard on me as many others. My mother-in-law had cancer and has since passed, but her immune system was very weak, so we were very protective. We stopped going to church for a while and started watching our services livestream, but we soon discovered that was way to convenient and becoming a habit.

Some reports I've read state that some churches are growing…online. There must be personal communication and interaction with others in the church body. I just don't believe you can have what God wanted for us when we gather together to worship Him on a TV or computer screen.

I opened with "does the church still have a pulse? Is there a better question to ask? How about, Why do so many refuse to believe in God or why do so many believe that God has no place or relevancy in our 21st century lives? Most current statistics say the average age of most church members is 58 and that we're losing the Millennium generation to no religious beliefs or church affiliations. Why is this, is it bad parenting, bad educational systems, bad churches or maybe a lot of lazy Christians.

We've gotten so set in our ways that all we do is come to Sunday school and church services, open our Bibles, sing a few hymns and then go home to a fine meal or a sports game. We've done what we believe is our personal responsibility, but church outreach, visiting, that's what the church staff is supposed to be doing not us.

We need a worldwide awakening, we need a revival in every American church, we need every Christian to be on fire to reach lost souls…I need the Holy Spirit to rekindle that fire in my soul for servant and service to others and to Almighty God. Does the church still have a pulse? Maybe the real question should be, do I still have a pulse, is my Christianity on life support?

2. **Evangelism, the church and the power of the pulpit**. Ok let's change gears for a moment. An entire book could be written on this subject and most likely there are several, but this is just some quick thoughts of mine. By the way I won't be referring to any minister I currently know in any of the following statements. I believe that the clear majority of ministers have a sincere heart for lost souls and are guided by the Holy Spirit in their messages and teachings. If this wasn't the case, believe me I would say so.

First let me say something about our technology and how it's used by some in the modern church. Today the American people are very much a mobile society. When I speak of mobility I'm not just talking about our cars, airplanes, or trains, I'm including our electronic technology. I'm confident that there are very few individuals in this country today that don't have access to computers or cellular smart phones. With the push of a few buttons or the click of a mouse we can go to just about anywhere on the planet via electronic means.

With my computer or my cell phone I was able to video call my daughter who was on the other side of the world for a few years. I can purchase just about anything needed for daily life over the internet without having to get dressed and go to someone's office or a store. Then within a day or two what I ordered will be on my front porch. These and other conveniences have become the daily norm whether they are for personal use, business, or entertainment.

Now, having said all of that what does this type of mobility and our technology have to do with the "modern Christian church?" How are they used by the church to reach people with the Word of GOD or how are they misguidedly used to grow the size and the wealth of just a few churches or a few individuals? Are today's church leaders focused on the right message? Are they properly using the technology to truly spread the whole Word of GOD and to reach as many lost souls as possible?

As I've stated even our small church has the ability to livestream our services online. There have to be thousands of churches doing the same thing but is it a good thing. For those that have health or mobility problems I would certainly say yes, but for the majority of us you need to be in fellowship with other like-minded Christians.

Let's first look at a few of the television or radio Evangelist. You almost always see and hear someone who has a very charismatic personality and is articulate in their message. They are presented in a large church auditorium (or studio) with a congregation the size of a small city. Their program is broadcast via TV or radio around the country or worldwide and the message seems to always be about hope, love, promises and forgiveness, which are very good Biblical truths. The reason I believe these are the predominant subjects chosen by Evangelists is because they are "feel good" messages that will bring about a more positive response by the listener. By that I mean both verbal and monetarily.

If I hear a message about GOD's judgement, hell, or something that hurts my conscious or really makes me feel bad about myself I'm more likely looking for the exit door or reaching for my TV remote control, not for my checkbook or wallet. My heart and soul may have needed that message, but it's not the word that would make me want to be generous with my money towards the one that delivered it.

Also, look at how they are utilizing the power of not just TV and radio, but the internet, DVD's and the sale of other items supposedly holding a religious meaning in order to generate revenue. Send me $25 and you'll receive a scented prayer cloth that will bless your life and heal whatever is bothering you.

I believe in some cases that this same reasoning also applies to our downtown or neighborhood churches. In many cases our large or so called mega-churches are organized and run more like a fortune five hundred corporation with more programs than the federal government. They have a "Senior Pastor" and his executive staff. I've even read of some mega-churches having a "board of directors" made up of elders and other influential members of the church and the local community.

The church is divided into several different operations and departments with "Pastors" in charge of each of those areas of the church. They will often have branch churches in the local community, in other states and sometimes even in other countries. Their Sunday morning service is highlighted by a Hollywood production of entertainment, music, skits, and church personalities. The have large choirs, praise singers, orchestras and bands, with a Jumbo Tron screen in case you're sitting in the back or in the balcony. Then a 15 minute speech that God loves everyone. Sadly, though I think too many of these mega-churches have or they are now focusing on their programs and numbers….dollars and donations….instead of prayer and salvation.

In many Sunday morning church services now days you have a 1-hour service where you get 20 to 30 minutes of announcements, music and entertainment followed by a 15 minute sermon. Somewhere in the hour we take up an offering that takes up another 5 minutes. Then we offer one or two verses of an invitational hymn for someone to come forward with a decision that will determine where they spend eternity. Now I know coming down in front of the church body doesn't save a person, it's just ironic that we spend more time in that 1 hour on donations and entertainment than we do on the message of salvation.

Then the congregation is dismissed with a parting prayer so they can beat the other neighborhood churches to the local restaurants or get home in time for the NFL kickoff. I know that many of us have a short attention span and that speakers will start to lose their audience after a certain period of time, but I think that GOD's Word and His messenger deserves the largest block of time in that hour.

Now that I've said these horrible things about the Evangelist and the churches in our country let me back up for a second. I don't really believe that all Evangelists are misguided, only a few, but like in most cases it only takes a few to give a bad impression about all the others. Are there some mega-churches doing good work for GOD and the community? Of course there are, and I believe that GOD can use any size of church to spread His message to His followers and the lost souls of our world. It's just that I believe sometimes the message and the individual can get lost in such a large church organization.

What I've seen on the other end of the spectrum is a growing number of home churches or Bible studies where small groups get together in a home or some other neutral location. Also, there has been a growing trend of non-denominational churches starting up in or near new subdivisions as they are built. Are these two groups more correctly focused on The Word of GOD, Salvation, and Christian growth of the people they minister to? I'm sure these groups are serving to spread the Gospel, provided they are being lead in solid Biblical truths and principals.

Now what is the "power of the pulpit?" Every time the President of the United States steps up to a podium to make a speech people listen. It doesn't make any difference whether you like or dislike, agree or disagree, you listen. Every time a leader of a state, a city government or the CEO of a major company makes a public speech, people listen. In religion, there have been many that when they stepped up to a podium in church or on a public square, people listened.

The Pope, the leader of the Catholic Church is always heard and scrutinized by millions of people every time he publicly speaks or issues a statement. The late Billy Graham for decades preached around the world and lead thousands to Christ. I believe people listened to him because he listened to GOD and let the Lord speak to the people through his voice and through the Holy Spirit.

The common thread with these people is that they came to the podium with the authority of their office and the power of something or someone higher than themselves, this is the "power of the pulpit." In one case, the law of the land and the people, and in the other, the Word of GOD and the Holy Spirit. The podium or the pulpit gives the speaker the location, the focal point, and the advantage to deliver their message.

One last thought on this subject. I believe that the pulpit's symbolically Holy Ground no matter if it's located in a church building, in a football stadium or in a plowed field. I get so mad when I see some activist or political figure in a church with some political speech or some rant about the police, the government or someone else. When the speaker steps up to the podium, I expect the Word of GOD to be proclaimed, not the speaker's politics. I hope that if my heart and my head is right with GOD, that the Holy Spirit will guide me to the proper decisions no matter what the spiritual, political, or personal issues are.

"I have wondered at times what the Ten Commandments would have looked like if Moses had run them through the U.S. Congress." Ronald Reagan [52]

3. <u>**Humans at their worst**</u>. A few years ago, I was watching a television news report about Islamic extremists and the beheading of some reporters and the question was where does this kind of hatred and behavior come from? I thought to myself, why is this such a big surprise to so many

people? Just look back at world history and tell me when there was a time or a culture somewhere in the world that was not guilty of some behavior and atrocities like this.

Even in America, look at how we treated the Native Indians and some of the disgusting ways we killed each other. You don't think that black slaves in this country were treated with Christian love, do you? How about the Chinese and how they were enslaved workers for the railroad and mining industries in the early American west?

I'm not condoning such actions by any means, it's all deplorable and should be condemned by any civilized society, but you can see such cruelty in almost any culture all the way back to early Biblical times. It was there with Cain and Able and it has been with us throughout history.

Listen to all the news reports after a terrorist attack and all the different reasons the various terrorist groups give for it happening. They don't mind being a martyr for Allah because they say that one of their rewards will be rivers of honey and 72 beautiful virgins. Even the women and children are willing to strap a bomb to themselves and commit suicide or take a gun or a knife and kill a specific target.

I know the infighting between Arab nations has been going on for thousands of years, but where does the modern day hatred of non-Muslims come from? Why is it so important to them that everyone convert to their beliefs and be subject to their laws and customs?

One day at work I was assigned to one of the airport terminals and as I was patrolling the upper curb area it suddenly dawned on me, most of our cab drivers are from the Middle East. Most of our bus drivers are from the Middle East. A very large number of the customer care and concession employees in the terminals are from the Middle East. I looked at the guys that drive the handicap carts or push the wheelchairs around the terminals and almost every one of them looks like they just stepped out of a Muslim temple in the Middle East. Even the contract security guards in the terminals are mostly from Middle Eastern countries.

Most of them are not American citizen's and I know this because I've worked in the airport badging office where you must present identification and theirs is always a Non-US passport and a Resident ID card. And if you ask them about citizenship, they have no intention of becoming U.S. citizens. Even some of our own security officers are from the Middle East or Central Africa. Many of them are making what is considered very good wages back in their own countries, so they are sending money home to support their family, or earning as much money as they can, before going home.

In 2014 who called for a "Jihad" against America and all the "unbelievers?" Tell me who's openly recruiting individuals for their cause right here in America? These people are not crazy; they're committed zealots and willing to die for their so called religion and its guiding principles. They're well organized and impressively financed. They have no deadlines, no elections, no constraints of law or rules of engagement. They only have one goal kill as many non-believers as possible and they are willing to die for their cause. This is a type of war that has been ongoing for thousands of years and it will still be going on when the rapture occurs.

4. **<u>Is this really a part of the Islamic Faith</u>**? Why won't those of the Muslim faith publicly condemn the actions of Islamic Terrorists? Should we even be asking that question? Dalia Mogahed, research director at the Institute for Social Policy and Understanding in Washington DC has answered that question with a convincing "no." During an interview on MSNBC, she was asked whether more Muslim leaders should speak out against ISIS. Here's her reply:

"I think we should take a step back and ask a different question, which is: 'Is it justified to demand that Muslims condemn terrorism?' Now that might sound a little radical even asking it. The reason I say that is this.

Condoning the killing of civilians is, to me, about the most monstrous thing you can do. And to be suspected of doing something so monstrous, simply because of your faith, seems very unfair.

When you look at the majority of terrorist attacks in the U.S., according to the FBI, the majority of domestic terror attacks are committed by white, male Christians. Now that's just the facts. When those things occur, we don't suspect other people who share their faith and ethnicity of condoning them. We assume these things outrage them just as much as they do anyone else. And we have to afford this same assumption of innocence to Muslims." [53]

Well, my rebuttal or answer to this question may not be politically correct, but here goes. Is it justified to demand that Muslims condemn terrorism? Yes, it's because ISIS is not claiming their actions are called for by some other religion, government power or some social club. I don't recall seeing too many Eskimos or Amish Elders on TV claiming responsibility or running terrorist training camps. I don't know if her FBI facts are correct, but for the sake of argument I will agree.

First, I don't know that these white males are really Christians, but even if they are, I haven't heard any of them claiming their actions are in accordance with their bible or what they perceive their religious faith tells them to do. If there was a group out there committing crimes in the name of the Bible I read or the church denomination I worship with, you bet I would be the first to stand up and condemn that group.

My point is that whatever they're claiming as their justification for their actions must be discredited and it must be done publicly and collectively by everyone. Who better to do that than the leaders and followers of the Islamic faith?

5. **<u>"I don't believe in GOD" "You can be your own GOD"</u>** You've heard them all and we know they're all lies. Humans are the only creatures in God's earthly creation that were given a soul or a spirit that without

question knows that there is a higher power, a Creator. Anyone that tells you that they don't believe in GOD, the Bible or a life after death has made a personal choice to believe that way and is choosing to deny or suppress what the human spirit is telling them.

I believe that the spirit in all of us is GOD's Holy Spirit telling each person, I'm here, I'm real, and that I want a relationship with you. God didn't create the universe and man so that he could just destroy it one day. Genesis 1:27 "So God created man in His own image; in the image of God He created him; male and female He created them."

Think about this, when a child is hungry, hurt or in need of some type of care who do they want? At an early age, they want their mother or father of course, because they instinctively know that is who all their needs, comfort, love, and security comes from.

I believe that in time of great fear, a severe trauma or at the moment of our death that the spirit that is within us, instinctively reaches out for our Creator, our Father, the one that provides all our needs, GOD. Or is that Him reaching in our hearts for us? Rev. William T. Cummings, served at Bataan, Philippines in WWII, and is famous for declaring ***"There are no atheists in foxholes."*** [54] I believe there are no atheists at the moment of our death and that the truth is revealed to everyone in the blink of an eye.

6. **<u>How do you know</u>**? Why is it that when we talk about someone who has died you always hear statements like, "he's not in pain anymore," or "she's in a better place now." We don't know any such thing. Only GOD Himself knows that; only He knows beyond any doubt the heart and soul of any individual. Unless that person accepted Jesus as Lord and Savior before the moment of their death I believe they are still suffering because they are not in a better place.

Witness to others when given the opportunity, pray for those in your life you love and care for before they pass on. Then if you believe they truly made that decision to accept God's free gift of salvation and you can see it in the way they live their lives then you can say "I believe he/she is with God now."

"Why is it that when we talk to God we're said to be praying, but when God talks to us, we're schizophrenic?" Lily Tomlin [55]

7. **Public Expression of Faith**! A coach prays before a game. An athlete points a finger toward Heaven or bows a knee in the end zone. Students voluntarily pray before a game or say our pledge of allegiance. These faithful people are increasingly being penalized or publicly ridiculed for showing their faith and giving glory to God. These simple acts of faith are now considered by some to be inappropriate or offensive to those of other religious beliefs. Would someone please tell me how this behavior could be considered improper or offensive in any setting?

A professional athlete beats his wife or girlfriend. An athlete or someone in public service uses drugs or gets drunk in public. Someone in the entertainment industry demonstrates some outrageous behavior either in their business or their public life. In all of these cases they get the minimum punishment by the law from inept liberal judges and they're still rewarded by those in their profession. For the most part the media condemns or ignores any expression of faith and is silent on the criminal or inappropriate behavior by those in Hollywood or high profile sports figures. God, I pray you give all Americans the sight to see how wrong these attitudes are and the courage to publicly stand against them.

"Freedom prospers when religion is vibrant and the rule of law under God is acknowledged." Ronald Reagan [56]

8. **In the name of "Allah."**   March 22, 2016, Brussels, Belgium. Several bombs were exploded in the airport and at two subway stations killing at least 26 people. In view of this deadly event what are we in America doing to protect our citizens? At DFW Airport we activated our Emergency Operations Center, police were in full riot gear, K-9 dogs were being taken for a walk through the terminals so the local media could see

them, and we put unarmed security officers walking the terminal curbs. A visual presence of uniform personnel will make the public feel safe and the activation of the EOC will play well in the media.

How stupid are we? No security measures could have stopped these bombings or any of the most recent killings, because they all happened in non-secure areas. We need to start at our borders and our ports of entry. We allow people to enter this country with very little effort, because we must be politically correct, and we can't offend anyone, and heaven forbid that we profile any individuals or groups. As I implied earlier on immigration, we need to close our borders, stop all immigration, start profiling where warranted, get control of who, how, where and when people are coming into this country. If we continue to demand political correctness and worry about how the rest of the world sees us, we'll soon be the direct target of these types of attacks, again. GOD help America.

9. **<u>Terror in America</u>**. Well let's answer the questions from the above entry. Terror has once again come to our shores and we are very stupid. Sunday morning, June 12, 2016 in Orlando, FL a self-proclaimed Islamic terrorist walks into a popular nightclub and opens fire with a semi-automatic weapon. When it's over the terrorist and 49 others are dead and 53 others receive various degrees of wounds from gunshots, flying debris or being trampled by crowds of people desperately trying to hide or escape the utter chaos all around them. The killer even stops during his rampage, calls 9-1-1 and claims responsibility for his actions in the name of ISIS. He also texts his wife to ask her if she knows what's going on. Then he reloads and resumes his murderous actions.

Omar Mateen, born in New York was an American and was being watched by the FBI. He had been interviewed at least twice by the FBI and even had ties to former terrorist. He had made at least two trips to Saudi Arabia and was able to recently purchase weapons with no problem. This is how stupid we are, and this tragedy is now the worst crime by a single gunman in our country's history. We must get smarter, tougher, and stop worrying about political correctness or what the rest of the world will think about us.

When I worked at DFW Airport I could make one phone call and in a matter of minutes I would know if you were on a watch list or if you are a person of serious concern. Why can't businesses that sell weapons do the same and if your name comes up you don't walk out any doors with a gun or any other serious weapons. Expand the Homeland Security Watchlist group into the already established regions around the country with operators 24/7 ready to run a computer identity check.

What is it going to take for government and law enforcement officials to take serious actions and stop worrying about offending someone or some group? I'm all about protecting our rights and freedoms, but you can't sit around and wait for guys like this to commit a crime before you do something.

10. **In the name of religion, really**! August 21, 2016. Many in the media and around the world are asking the questions, "what kind of religion encourages and celebrates martyrdom?" "what kind of person straps a bomb to a woman or a small child?" I really don't know if there is any established religion that believes such things, but I do believe there are some sick and disturbed individuals within the Islamic faith that are using their religious beliefs as a platform for some barbaric actions.

Over the last couple of months there have been several devastating bombings in Turkey, with the most recent one being at a wedding celebration. It's reported that a child between the age of 12 to 14 walked in the building with a bomb strapped to himself and set it off in the middle of a group of dancers. The Turkish President stated that at present 51 adults and children are dead and another 69 were in the hospital with 17 of them "heavily injured." Other reports say they're in critical condition.

What can you say about these types of people? I'm so tired of them hurting people all over the world and getting headlines. I'm almost to the point that just maybe we need a coalition of countries and just go over there and bomb the whole middle east back to the stone age, except I think most people living there are still in the stone age. If the honest Muslims and faithful of the Islamic faith don't start speaking up every chance they get to condemn these terrorists I'm afraid that a lot of people are going to condemn them right along with the Islamic terrorists. I'm so tired of hearing about them, talking and writing about them. GOD, please restrain them and deliver us from this evil.

SECTION NINE
THE GOOD OLD DAYS

This section is all about that walk down memory lane. The things I remember about being a kid growing up in North Texas and the joy of childhood. Remembering some events in history that have a special meaning to me and how our lives have changed over the years.

1. **What were the "Good Old Days?"** How many times have you heard someone say that they missed the "good old days?" That they missed the way things used to be when they were growing up or when they were young adults. I started thinking about all the changes and advances we have had in the last 100 to 150 years or just the technological changes in my lifetime. What exactly were the good old days? Was it a specific period of time or was it just a state of mind when we looked at things much differently?

Were the good old days before doctors had medical treatments and the modern medicines that eliminated many serious afflictions and deadly diseases in most advanced countries? Were the good old days the ones before doctors could perform the miracles of organ transplants or micro-surgery that added years or even decades to our lives? How about the advances in prosthetics that allows a person to do many of the things they did before losing a limb?

Were the good old days when it took months for a letter to get across the country? I like being able to send an instant message to my friends and family no matter where they're located on the globe. I like being able to pull a cell phone out of my pocket and calling someone no matter where they are or placing an order for something that will arrive in just a few hours or a few days.

Were the good old days when it took all day to get to town and back by walking dirt roads in all types of weather; with a wagon and a pair of mules or a Model-T Ford? I like being able to get in my vehicle no matter what the weather conditions are, or the price of gas and being able to drive to the local Wal-Mart, Home Depot or to work and back on the same day and in time for supper.

Were the good old days when you cut wood to cook your meals and heat your home in the winter or sweat like crazy in the summer plowing the fields to grow your own food or tending livestock for meat? I like my all electric house with central air and heat, my electric range that heats up with the turn of a knob and all the other conveniences regardless of how much I fuss about the utility bills.

I'm not a farmer or a rancher and I don't live on a dairy, so I like getting my food from the neighborhood Kroger Store. I like getting just a gallon of milk or picking can goods and bread off the shelves instead of milking cows every morning or waiting for the right time to pick my vegetables out of the ground. And if I don't want to cook at home I get in my car and in less than an hour I can be seated eating a hamburger, seafood or a steak dinner in a nice restaurant.

The good ole days that I grew up in had some fun things like the dances we called "sock-hops," roller skating rinks on hardwood floors under a tent or double features at a drive-in movie. Boys driving their hot-rods up and down the strip trying to impress the girls.

But today I like the entertainment of HDTV with programs on demand, DVD's, and satellite radio where you can listen to the same channel across the country. I like this computer I'm using and cell phones that work from almost anywhere on the globe. I like how modern inventions have made daily life more enjoyable when they're used responsibly and for their intended purpose. I remember my good old days and from the standpoint of things that enrich our daily lives I'll take these better days of the twenty-first century.

2. <u>We have liftoff</u>. I grew up during the "space race" and I miss the excitement of the early days in the American space program. So much of the technology and advancements we have now were born from the research and development during the space program. Yes, it's good that private companies are now taking the lead and getting into space research, but it seemed that nothing could beat the collective efforts of the American people and in my opinion one of the best government agencies ever created, the National Aeronautics and Space Administration, NASA.

Back then we knew their names; Alan Shepard, John Glen, Gus Grissom, Gordon Cooper, Scott Carpenter, Wally Schirra and Deke Slayton, they were America's first Mercury Astronauts. Every time one of them went up we were all glued to the TV. Where are the heroes of space travel today? They're there, we just don't hear about them, after all America doesn't even have a spaceship now that all the shuttles have been retired. We don't even have our own rocket engines; we buy them from the Russians! When we send our astronauts to the international space station they have to go up in a Russian spaceship. When will we get another ship?

Well it just so happens that we landed a new rover on Mars on February 18, 2021. The rover Perseverance took 203 days to make the journey from earth and then entered the Martian atmosphere at 12,000 mph. The landing craft fired its engines to slow the decent and at about 1 mile up the parachute deployed. Minutes after landing on the Martian surface the Perseverance started sending back pictures. The rover even carried a new mini rotorcraft that will launch and take pictures of the surface from an elevated view. The main mission of the project is to seek signs of ancient life and collect samples of rock and regolith (broken rock and soil) for possible return to Earth. This is all very exciting to me, but I like many others still ask the question, when will "man" travel back to the moon or to another planet?

3. <u>Play Ball</u>! Here's something many of us might really miss. When I was growing up baseball was king, and every boy played on a little league team or in a back lot. This was the era of "Baseball, hotdogs and mom's apple pie." We had snow cones, cotton candy and we always had a mouth full of pink bubble gum. Our baseball card collections included the likes of Willie Mays, Mickey Mantle, Roger Maris, Henry "Hank" Aaron, Stan Musial and of course the great Ted Williams.

The season started with us getting together and forming teams with whatever number of kids we had. It was Saturday mornings going to the ball field or the field behind our house. When you were old enough and you got to be on a city little league team you had made the big league! After your first game, somehow you were now a baseball expert and if you got a home run or made a big play you were a neighborhood hero. And of course, if your team won the game your parents always told the neighbor that you saved the game despite the bad calls by the umpires.

For me it was also fun listening to the games on the family radio or sitting around in the garage if your dad had it on the portable Philco or RCA radio. If we could catch a game on TV that was a real treat even if it was only a black and white screen. I remember the excitement of seeing a home run by your favorite player and yes, I even remember the commercials. Gillette shaving razors and blades, Wheaties or Corn Flakes Cereal, Coca-Cola or Dr Pepper's 10-2-4.

Almost every boy had a baseball card collection that we kept in shoe boxes, card file boxes or whatever worked best. We knew every player. We knew the teams they played on and could tell you how many home runs they had and what a player's season batting average was. Right or wrong we looked up to and treated the players like heroes and I don't recall ever hearing bad things about them like you do now days. I'm not naive to think it wasn't there, but I think the standards of media coverage was very different back then.

Yes, I'm dreaming of springtime again as I write this entry and that means baseball, T-Ball, coach pitch, little league, pony league, select teams, so many different names and levels. But no matter what you call it, and no matter what the age, it's still a bat, a ball, a glove, and a childhood dream of hitting the game winning home run. It's a dream that all children can have, and adults can still remember.

4. <u>Great TV shows of the past</u>. What were the best television shows in your past that had you glued to the TV every time they came on? I go back a ways to the days of the first run series of "Gunsmoke." I can remember staying overnight at my grandfather's house and he would get the sofa bed in the living room made out and I would lay there watching Matt Dillon with my grandfather.

As a family I remember watching shows like "I love Lucy," "The Honeymooners" "The Ed Sullivan Show" and game shows like "What's My Line" from the 1950's. Later came shows like "The Andy Griffith Show" "The Dick Van Dyke Show" and the country music show "Hee Haw." And of course you can't forget "Leave It To Beaver." All of these were good clean family shows that any age could watch and enjoy.

In the 1970's it was shows like "M*A*S*H" "All In The Family" "Sanford and Son" or "The Mary Tylor Moore Show." These shows would entertain you and make you laugh, but they were also some bold groundbreaking scripts taking on the social issues of the day.

Of course none of these shows were explicit in bad language, sex or violence. In most of the early ones you hardly saw the couples in bed and in most of the shows back then couples slept in separate beds. M*A*S*H and All In The Family started to push the boundary lines, but to me they were still in the "G" rated category.

These were just a few of the shows I watched as a youth and young adult that take me back to a different time that left me with some very good memories, and some are shows that I still watch in reruns today.

5. **<u>Great movie memories</u>**. I watched one of the all-time classic movies, "Hoosiers." Now everyone sees things like a movie differently, because we all have different interest and different values. I saw this movie as a superb story about second chances, teamwork, faith, discipline, sobriety, and self-control. These life lessons make Hoosiers one of the most inspirational stories about life in rural America you will ever watch. It's the story of victory and how a small rural high school basketball team overcame all odds and immerged not just as the state champions in a sport, but also in life. A story of faith and how one's prayers can be answered. It's the story of rebuilding lives.

The movie follows the residents of Hickory, Indiana exhibiting in several characters that no matter what your lot in life is, there is the chance of redemption, a second chance for success, a second chance in changing the direction of your life. The main characters are a coach that had lost a promising career at the college level and a teacher that finds a second chance at love. A father that gets another chance at getting sober and changing his life, while his son learns love and forgiveness. And a whole town that finds out that there are more important things than winning.

Another great movie I recently saw for the first time "The Railway Man." The movie stars Colin Firth and Nicole Kidman and is based on a true story of a British couple dealing with the harsh memories of World War II. Firth portrays a former WWII lieutenant who is still trying to deal with the memories of being a POW tortured by the Japanese military following the fall of Singapore in 1942.

Firth's character Eric Lomax won't open up and talk to his wife Patti, played by Kidman, so she seeks to learn about the war years from her husband's long-time friend and fellow POW Finley played by Stellan Skarsgård. During the war, the Japanese army constructed the Burma-Siam Railway. It's believed that hundreds of thousands of Asian laborers, and 60,000 allied prisoners of war were forced to build the line. It became known as the Death Railway. The book and the movie "The Bridge Over the River Kwai" are loosely based on the real story of the Death Railway.

The performances by everyone were outstanding and conveyed all the strong emotions of fear, pain, evil and then regret and forgiveness. The story follows Lomax as he returns to the POW camp finding that the Japanese army officer, Nagase, that served as an interrupter and was involved in most of his torture is now profiting by running the camp as a war museum.

As Lomax confronts Nagase seeking revenge he is once again tortured by all of the memories and also finds that Nagase is really trying to find peace and forgiveness for his actions. The movie shows that they both found some measure of peace and reconciliation and became good friends for the remainder of their lives. I found this to be an excellent movie displaying the real horrors of war and the invisible lifelong scars and effects. I strongly recommend this movie as it's now one of my favorites.

Where are the classic movies like they use to make, such as these "Hoosiers" and "The Railway Man" or "Gone with the Wind," "Mary Poppins," "The Ten Commandments," "It's a Wonderful Life," "State Fair" or "She Wore a Yellow Ribbon." I realize that the cost of making big movies has gone up tremendously, but I love the family feel good and the big epic movies of the past. I know that most movies and many TV shows have gotten too graphic with sex, death and destruction. Watch a good clean family movie from the golden age of Hollywood or if you can't do that, read a good story from the Bible, they're just as exciting and they're true.

6. <u>**No one talks like that**</u>. Speaking of good old movies, I was watching one the other day and I started to notice the language the actors were using, and I wondered if that was the way people really spoke during the time period that was being depicted. In this case it was the decades that followed the U.S. Civil War. When a man was introduced to a woman he would always reply "your servant mam." Other expressions included "It would be my pleasure," "with your permission," or how about this one "my respects sir."

When people signed a personal letter it might be something like "I am and will always be your loving son," or "Your faithful and loving husband." Now days all we send is text messages or emails with incorrect grammar and end them with "LOL," now isn't that real personal! Why can't we still be more expressive today? Are our lives so "time crunched" so segmented that we can't take time to be polite, to have an actual conversation or relationship with one another? Put a pen in your hand and see if you can still write. Send a handwritten letter to someone, they just might be excited to get it and they just might enjoy reading what you have to say. Try earning others respect and use "yes sir" or "no mam" or how about "I would love to help you." Sign a letter with "Respectfully" or "In Christ." Good manners are enjoyed by everyone.

7. **<u>That's old music Grandpa</u>**! Now, let me transition from film and language to music. Just as I have wondered about my grandparents I'll bet generations from now someone reading this might ask, "well what kind of music did Great Grandpa David listen to back in the old days." Well right now I always love a good old song out of the Baptist hymnal or some Gospel toe tapping music, but I also like to listen to today's Country Music hits by Blake Shelton, Brad Paisley or maybe Toby Keith.

Growing up in the 1950's and 60's the new music back then was, Rock 'n Roll, Doo Wop, Rhythm and Blues and Folk music. It seemed like every week there was a new artist like Otis Redding, Elvis Presley, Chubby Checker, Chuck Berry, or Jerry Lee Lewis. Groups like The Beach Boys, The Beatles, The Coasters, The Dave Clark Five or The Drifters. Of course there were hundreds of others during that 20+ year period and a lot of what they called "One Hit Wonders." Even today I like to listen to the "oldies" on occasion.

8. <u>**Are we there yet**</u>?   What has happened to the good ole family vacation? When I was growing up a family vacation was everyone piling into the family station wagon, pulling a trailer or camper behind it and heading for the mountains or the lake. My Dad loved to fish so most of our weekends and vacations were spent south of Fort Worth at Lake Whitney where we had a mobile home and a cabin boat. Those were great times and gave me many more family memories than a stay at the Holiday Inn Express would have. Unless you were rich, you didn't fly off to the Caribbean, Mexico, Hawaii or maybe to Europe.

Families got away and spent time together and enjoyed doing some of the simplest of activities. Today it seems that it's not a vacation unless everyone can fly off to Cancun, the Bahamas, or Disney World and of course the kids take their cell phones and video games with them. I think parents even look for opportunities to ship the kids off somewhere separate while Mom and Dad take their own vacation.

Come on parents take the family to the beach, mountains, the lake or go camping. Go see some historical monuments like Mount Rushmore or take in all the history of Washington D.C. Just take the time to spend it somewhere with your children and enjoy each other's company, create some fun memories and be a family. Your children will look back and thank you later when they're doing the same thing with their own family.

9. <u>Let us be thankful and give praise to God</u>.   This entry is from November 26, 2015, Thanksgiving Day and as you read this, you're asking yourself why he is writing on a holiday and not spending time with the family. Well the answer is I'm at work at DFW Airport, but there is not much going on where I'm working today, and there has to be someone to earn all of that big holiday pay. I'll be with the family later and we'll be having our big dinner and get together on Saturday.

Getting back on topic, I wonder if we as Americans are truly thankful for the blessings, joys and freedoms we have inherited from the generations before us. Do we are our children even understand the meaning of Thanksgiving? During my childhood I remember that no matter where we lived or how poor we might have been, we always managed to celebrate Thanksgiving with an extra special meal. However I don't remember counting my blessings or ever giving a lot of thought to freedoms and liberty we enjoyed as Americans.

As kids I'm not sure we knew exactly what to be thankful for, except good food and leftovers. I can still see and smell those turkeys Mom would cook. One thing I have always loved is a honey cured ham. I could eat my weight in ham along with mash potatoes and gravy, and my current weight proves it. Of course there was all the other items that were included along with some great dinner rolls, but as kids you know what we were waiting for, those pies! Families have all kinds of different deserts, but for us it was always the traditional pumpkin and pecan pies. I couldn't get enough pecan pie!

Today as a look back I know exactly what I was blessed to have, because "hindsight is 20/20." I won't dwell on family history, you will have to read my autobiography when I'm finished with that, I will simply say that I'm grateful for the family we were. The small things that we had, such as a roof over our heads or money for food and clothing. The love and devotion we shared, for what we were blessed to have in hard times and good. I know we didn't think of Life, Liberty and Freedom and the price that was paid by thousands of men and women in previous generations.

After I got married I was blessed with my wife, Cheryl that she could cook and got even better every year. The traditional foods continued, and we started making our own Thanksgiving customs. I learned how to carve a turkey and that became my job. I guess because I was a sailor peeling potatoes and making mash potatoes also became a cooking chore of mine.

One of the traditions we started doing was inviting some of the sailors I was stationed with to share Thanksgiving Day dinner with us. This was other families we were close friends with and some of the single guys and gals that had no family with them and were not going home for the holidays.

There were a couple of times we may have had as many as 10 to 15 people over for dinner. Depending on the weather we might have a touch football game out front or just play with the kids before the big meal, then of course there was the big NFL game on TV and lying in the floor or on the couch because we ate too much. I hope we were a blessing to some of those young folks that came over and that we made them feel like family.

These were great times that I'm truly thankful for. I worry about today's families and the observance of the holiday itself. Is the holiday being lost in all the commercial hype? It's almost like we go straight from dressing up in costumes and going to parties for Halloween to putting out our Christmas lights.

Is the holiday itself and the meaning of it slowly losing its traditional place with the American family? I've observed that many restaurants aren't closing on Thanksgiving and more families are going out to just have a nice dinner. How many Americans could tell you the history or the true meaning of "Thanksgiving?" For many of us, the meaning of Thanksgiving usually includes feasting, four-day weekends, the football games, or family reunions.

The first Thanksgiving was neither a feast nor a holiday, but it was a simple gathering. The Mayflower had arrived at Plymouth Rock on December 11, 1620, the Pilgrims suffered the loss of 46 of their original 102 colonists. With the help of the native Indians, the surviving Pilgrims then suffered a bitter winter, but had a bountiful harvest in 1621. In celebration, a traditional English harvest festival, lasting three days brought the Pilgrims and natives to unite in a "thanksgiving" observance.

It wasn't until June 1676 that another "thanksgiving meal" would be observed. On June 29th, the community of Charlestown, Mass. proclaimed a day of thanksgiving for their good fortune. This time there were no Indians, the colonists' celebrating victory over the "heathen natives." The celebration would not be observed again for one hundred years, in October 1777, with all 13 colonies participating in a one-time "thanksgiving" celebration. This time the celebration commemorated their victory over the British at Saratoga. It wasn't until 1789 President George Washington proclaimed it to be a national holiday and in 1863 President Lincoln was convinced to declare the last Thursday in November as a day of "Thanksgiving." It wouldn't be until 1941 that Congress would sanction it as a legal holiday.

The meaning of our Thanksgiving celebration has undergone many changes. An expression of gratitude for survival; a community's recognition of its flourishing growth; the defeat over the British for our freedom and the beginning of a new nation. Over time we have all added our own customs, preserving those that are most meaningful to us.

The Holy Bible tells us in Nehemiah 12:27 that the meaning of "thanksgiving" reflected adoration, sacrifice, praise, or an offering. Thanksgiving was a grateful language to GOD as an act of worship. Long before the colonists celebrated their successes, Nehemiah assembled two great choirs to give thanks for GOD's faithfulness in rebuilding the wall.

The true meaning of Thanksgiving focuses on a relationship between GOD and man. Upon their arrival at New Plymouth, the Pilgrims were quick to honor GOD with, The Mayflower Compact, acknowledging GOD as faithful, and earnestly giving Him thanks in advance for His abundant blessings. Thanksgiving is an attitude of the heart that reinforces an intimate relationship with GOD.

Now why have I spent so much time on this subject, obviously because I think it's an important subject. It concerns me that American families, blessed with so many riches and freedoms are losing sight of all the abundant blessings GOD has showered on this country and on each of us collectively as a nation.

We should be thankful to all those patriots, both in and out of uniform, that have come before us and that now serve us. Those that have given so much of themselves to secure and keep safe the freedoms and the ideals we declare to be so precious to us. We should be thankful for our families; all the love that binds us together and support that they provide us. Most important, let our "thanksgiving" each day be a grateful language of praise and adoration to GOD and may we all reflect the true meaning and spirit of the day.

Philippians 4:6. "In everything, by prayer and petition, with thanksgiving, present your requests to GOD" [57]

10. <u>The news, then and now</u>. I remember the television evening news that my parents had to see every day. It was like a ritual, no matter what was happening it would have to wait until after the news. Back then, the late 1950's and 1960's, there was only three networks, ABC, CBS and NBC and TV personalities like Walter Cronkite, David Brinkley, and Chet Huntley. These were journalists that knew how to get to the heart of a news story, deliver the facts, not their personal opinions.

It was like that line from the old TV show Dragnet when the detective says, "just the facts ma'am." The news was not a popularity contest; it was a trust. Who could the viewers trust to hear the whole story, with just the facts? Not the editorial or the personal opinion of the reporter. They didn't tell you what to believe but left many conclusions up to the viewer.

Speaking of editorials, I remember the last two or three minutes of the broadcast was called the "Editorial Segment." This is when the news anchor, the news director or a guest would deliver a news story with their personal opinion, but most of the time they would leave it up to the viewer to draw their own conclusion. These were professional journalist that knew and understood it was all about the facts of the story and not about the reporter; get it first but get it right.

As television and TV news became increasingly more popular throughout the 1960's, writers reacted with the creation of a "new journalism" based largely on literary technique and first-person accounts. The goal being network ratings, advertising dollars and awards. News anchors have always reported from the field depending on the event, such as the Viet Nam War. Today they make a big deal about news anchors and reporters that are "imbedded" with combat forces in the field. As a former military leader I probably would have told any reporter with my unit, "you've got the point" as we moved into the battle.

As this practice increased the news became increasingly about the person delivering the story, than about the story itself. Today's network news broadcasts are full of personal bias and political punditry; it's more about an effective presentation, the social implications, or the political consequences and much less about those involved and the facts of the original story.

11. <u>Cleared for takeoff</u>. I've been around aviation almost my entire life and it's amazing how much it has evolved in the past 100 years or just the past 30 years that I've been associated with the industry. I remember before I was a teenager running around Greater Southwest International Airport while my uncle was working in his office or the control tower back in the late 1950's.

When I first entered the Navy I became a Navy Air Traffic Controller and we still used raw radar and paper maps on the wall or desk to keep track of aircraft. Now we have sophisticated computers keeping track of hundreds of aircraft at the same time and real time movement data maintained and displayed on the radar screen. I once described it to a lady "it's the best and most expensive video game in the world, just keep the little dots from hitting one another." She was sitting next to me on an airplane!

Aircraft have gone from single engine piston driven aircraft to four engine jets that are double decker's and carry up to 500 passengers, like the new Airbus A380. Passenger planes have gone from flying only several hundred miles non-stop to cruising miles high in comfort halfway around the earth non-stop. From flying only several thousand feet up, because of the lack of air pressure and the need for oxygen, aircraft with pressurized cabins that can fly seven miles high. Military jets can fly sub-orbital several times faster than the speed of sound.

What this entry is about is the people that travel. About a memorable period that we'll never see again. For the past eight years, I've worked at DFW Airport and I love to observe people and this airport is a great place to do exactly that.

If you look back in aviation history, you'll find from the 1940's through the 1960's flying was something special and when people did fly they dressed up for it as if it was a big social event. Men always wore suits or at least dress slacks and a nice shirt. Women worn their Sunday dress and of course their hats. Hats of every type, size, and color. Children were dressed appropriately and behaved (most of the time) like little ladies and gentlemen.

Today it's gym gear, torn jeans and sometimes I think their sleepwear. Air travel today is available to just about everyone across the social and economic spectrum. And yes, I will say it, there are some low class rednecks that should be going by bus or in their own pickup truck instead of sitting 4 inches from another passenger and smelling like they just slopped the hogs. You may not like the fact that I just said that, but you'll understand if you ever sit next to a person in that enclosed environment for several hours and they have yet to discover soap or underarm deodorant!

In the more romantic days of air travel there was no TSA and in larger airports it was the city police that patrolled the airport. There may have been some security officers at certain locations. Other than airline personnel, the uniforms you saw the most of was U.S. Customs Officers in the international airports. With the deregulation of the airline industry and all the discount airlines and airline programs, air travel is affordable and available to so many more people these days, but this also creates many more problems.

The conduct of air passengers now days never ceases to amaze me. When I worked at DFW Airport not a day would go by that we didn't have numerous police calls for irate passengers yelling at airline or TSA personnel for some reason. We have a small jail at the airport and almost daily we will have several passengers locked up, mostly for public intoxication, but some are for assault or individuals that have arrest warrants on them from other cities.

There are cases every day of lost or stolen bags and personal items. We have human trafficking of women and children, lost children and the elderly, traffic problems and vehicle wrecks. And of course, as in any large population we have multiple medical calls every day from small cuts to major traumas, heart attacks and even deaths.

Unfortunately, there is the chance of terrorist threats or actions that could have devastating results. DFW Airport is the size of a major city that grew up in the fields and farmland between Dallas and Fort Worth Texas and we have a lot of the same problems of a large city when it comes to security and emergency services. Everyone in security and law enforcement are constantly training and changing procedures as the threats change. To me it's very sad that air travel has become so stressful for those that travel and those that provide the services.

12. <u>**True Love**</u>. I think I've already made it obvious that I'm a Ronald Reagan (1911-2004) fan and that I remember the Reagan presidential years with fondness and great respect. Those were good years for me, my naval career, and my family. On the morning of Monday March 7, 2016, we learned of the passing of his beloved wife Nancy.

Over the years there have been several stories about her and the influence she had over policy decisions, speeches and how the White House and the staff were run. Many believed that Nancy was the one you had to go through in order to have access to the President, including those in the media to ranking government officials. I don't know how many of those stories are true, but I believe that she was a very influential first lady and that the stories about her love and devotion to her husband were all absolutely true.

For 52 years, she was always at his side even into his years of declining health. Their life together in Hollywood, the California Governor's mansion, to the highest office in the land and then home to their ranch in California has become an American love story recorded in several books and film documentaries. Nancy once said, "My life didn't really begin until I met Ronnie."

Rarely was there ever a picture that Nancy wasn't at his side or somewhere very close by. There have been many stories about their love and devotion for each other including how she continued to speak and write about him and how she was involved in the management of the Reagan Library in California. Even at her televised funeral everyone that spoke talked about her strong love and devotion to her husband. No matter what her faults may have been, Nancy Reagan was a lady of class and distinction and will be missed by many in this country and around the world. For now though, I hope she is with the Lord and with her "Ronnie."

13. <u>An American Icon</u>. I spoke earlier in this section about my love of NASA, the space program, my admiration of the early astronauts and now this entry from December 8, 2016. It was just announced that John Glenn has died at the age of 95. Astronaut John Glenn, one of the original 7 American Astronauts had great careers in the military, NASA, and the U.S. Senate. He was the last of America's original Mercury Astronauts.

Mr. Glenn was a Marine Fighter Pilot in World War II flying 59 missions over enemy targets in the South Pacific. Later in Korea he flew his F9F Panther in 63 combat missions, gaining the nickname "magnet ass" from his alleged ability to attract enemy flak. It's reported that on two separate occasions, he returned to his base with over 250 holes in his aircraft. For a few missions, he flew with Marine reservist Ted Williams (future Baseball Hall of Famer) as his wingman. Glenn later entered the military test pilot program and on July 16, 1957, Glenn recorded the first supersonic transcontinental flight from California to New York in a Vought F8U-3P Crusader in 3 hours and 23 minutes.

As one of America's first astronauts, Glenn just barely met the requirements for the program. He was almost 40 years old, the cut off age, and lacked a science based college degree. During NASA's Mercury program, he only flew in space once, and all the while he was still on active duty with the Marine Corps.

Glenn resigned from NASA on January 16, 1964, and the next day announced his candidacy for the U.S. Senate from his home state of Ohio. However, he suffered a concussion from a fall against a bathtub and this required him to withdraw from the race. Still on duty with the Marine Corps, Glenn went on convalescent leave until he could make a full recovery and then retire from the Marines. He retired on January 1, 1965, as a full Colonel and became an executive for Royal Crown Cola.

In 1970, Glenn was narrowly defeated in the Ohio primary for the U.S. Senate. In 1974, Glenn rejected Ohio governor and the Ohio Democratic party's demand that he run for Lieutenant Governor. Instead, Glenn ran and won the Democratic primary and then defeated Ralph Perk, the Republican Mayor of Cleveland in the general election, beginning a Senate career that would span twenty five years until his retirement in 1999.

Glenn returned to space on the Space Shuttle, October 29, 1998, as a Payload Specialist on Discovery's STS-95 mission, becoming at age 77 the oldest person to go into space. According to some critics Glenn received his seat on the Shuttle flight by lobbying NASA for two years to fly as a human guinea pig for geriatric studies. Also, many believed it was a political favor granted to Glenn by President Clinton. Upon the safe return of the STS-95 crew, Glenn (and his crewmates) received a ticker-tape parade, making him the tenth, and latest person to have received multiple ticker-tape parades in a lifetime. Besides his military medals and many honors received by John Glenn, he has also been awarded the Congressional Gold Medal, the Presidential Medal of Freedom, and the Congressional Space Medal of Honor.

A spokesman for Ohio State University announced on Wednesday December 7, 2016 Senator Glenn had been hospitalized for over a week. His illness was not disclosed. Glenn's death was announced Thursday by officials at Ohio State University, where he was being treated. Glenn had experienced a number of health problems in recent years, including a stroke he suffered two years ago, after having had heart valve replacement surgery. Glenn's body will lie in state at the Ohio Statehouse for one day and he is to be buried in a private service at Arlington National Cemetery.

Through the years, I disagreed strongly with most of Glenn's politics, but I truly admired the man for his military career and for his bravery as a pilot and in the U.S. space program. I am very saddened by the passing of one of our nation's pioneers.

SECTION TEN
WHERE WERE YOU WHEN

In this section, I'm looking at historical events that had a defining moment in our country or our lives. If you were alive then, what were you doing. Did any of these effect or influence your life?

1951: This was the year I was born, so of course I don't remember anything, but it was the year that a color TV program was first broadcast. It wasn't until the 1970s that the American public finally started purchasing more color TV sets than black-and-white.

1957: On October 4th the world is surprised when the Russians launched the first satellite "Sputnik" to orbit the earth. I remember the event, but I don't know what I was doing when the news hit the media. It was a 22 inches in diameter and 183 lbs. It reached an orbit height of 359 miles.

1960: The presidential race to succeed President Dwight D. Eisenhower is won by the Democratic candidate, Senator John F. Kennedy over the incumbent Vice President Richard M. Nixon. Of course, I was still a little kid then, but for some reason I remember the election and I remember the TV debate with Richard Nixon. It might be because we watched so much TV together as a family and of course Dad was the one that decided most of the time what we were watching.

1961: Like baseball I loved everything about the space program. The Russians had the first human in space, but on Friday May 5th, 1961 Astronaut Alan Shepard became the first American launched into space. Liftoff was at 9:34 AM and the flight lasted only 15 minutes. This first successful launch in the American Astronaut program was a huge milestone and I believe gave us the courage and the drive to go forward.

It was called the "space race" and after President Kennedy's speech to put a man on the moon it truly was a race. I was in front of a TV every chance I got to watch every launch and whatever else was going on. Some of our teachers even had TV's in their classrooms so we wouldn't miss a launch or a recovery. I think all Americans were fascinated by the idea of going into space and couldn't get enough of watching history as it was made.

1961: On August 5th the new theme park Six Flags over Texas officially opens to the public. The best I remember the only theme park on this same level was Disneyland in Anaheim, CA. My Dad didn't like being in large crowds, but as I look back it was a surprise to me that he took the family to Six Flags the first week it opened. I remember that day clearly and we had a great time. Even Dad got on a few of the tamer rides and I know Mom got on the log ride with us. The prices, then and now, are simply amazing to me.

Opening Day August 5, 1961	2021 Season Gate Price
Adult Ticket $2.75	$79.99

1963: On Friday, November 22, Dallas Texas, John F. Kennedy, 35th President of the United States of America is shot in downtown Dallas. At 1:00 PM the president is pronounced dead at Parkland Hospital. The transition of power cannot wait. At 2:38 PM the Vice President, Lyndon B. Johnson is given the oath of office as the 36th President onboard Air Force One.

We had just come back from lunch when an announcement was made on the school's public address system, the president and Texas Governor, John Connelly had been shot. My teacher had a radio in the back of the classroom. He turned it on WBAP, and we spent the next couple of hours listening to all the reports.

That weekend I stayed glued to the TV. Like many Americans I too couldn't get enough of the Kennedy's and you felt the sorrow for Mrs. Kennedy and the children. The news coverage continued for days and months with many different reasons for the assassination. I remember so many things I saw on TV during the days leading up to the funeral and how sad our country was. These were some dark days in our history.

1964: The Beatles make their American television debut on the "The Ed Sullivan Show." The following morning practically every newspaper in the U.S. wrote that the Beatles were nothing more than a "fad," and they "couldn't carry a tune across the Atlantic." I can still see as Ed Sullivan came back from commercial, introduced the Beatles and they began to play. I was hooked on their music, but as my Dad watched Ringo on the drums using a simple beat, Dad said as he moved his hands to the music, *"I can do that!"* Dad had a musical background, but it was the slide trombone.

1969: July 16th, 9:32 p.m. CST Apollo 11 lifts off launch pad 39A at the Kennedy Space Center. Onboard the spacecraft is Neil Armstrong, Michael Collins, and Edwin "Buzz" Aldrin Jr. Four days later Armstrong and Aldrin landed the lunar module Eagle safely on the surface of the moon becoming the first humans on another world.

I was glued to the TV like millions around the world and I heard Armstrong's now famous words ***"Houston, Tranquility Base here, the Eagle has landed."*** And later ***"that's one small step for [a] man, one giant leap for mankind"*** as he leaped from the lunar module ladder to the surface of the moon. He forgot the "a" before man.

1970: April 11, at 1:13 p.m. CST Apollo 13 lifts off launch pad 39A at the Kennedy Space Center just 9 months after the moon landing of Apollo 11. The crew was James A. Lovell Jr., Commander; Fred W. Haise Jr., Lunar Module Pilot; and John L. Swigert Jr., Command Module Pilot. At 5.5 minutes into the launch they felt a vibration and the center engine shut down 2 minutes early.

At 55 hours, 46 minutes into the flight, as the crew finished a 49-minute TV broadcast oxygen tank No. 2 blew up, causing the No. 1 tank to also fail. The command module's normal supply of electricity, light and water was lost, and they were about 200,000 miles from Earth. The crew was in dire trouble loosing oxygen in the command module and after moving to the Land Module (LM) they were accumulating more carbon dioxide than the human body could take because the O2 scrubbers that cleaned the air had failed and the square filters from the command module were not compatible with the round ones in the LM.

All of these problems were temporarily fixed and the spacecraft had continued around the moon and was now heading back to earth. But wait there was more to worry about, was the heat shield on the command module damaged during the explosion? As it turns out it was fine and the crew returned safely to earth landing in the Pacific Ocean on April 17. Although they didn't land on the moon the mission was classified as "A Successful Failure" because of all that was learned about equipment, procedures and man's endurance in space.

1972: August 4th the date of my wedding to the precious gift that God had for me. I couldn't leave this one out.

1974: August 5th Following the Watergate break-in and subsequent cover-up by the administration, President Richard M. Nixon became the first U.S. President to resign from office before completing his term. Mr. Nixon made public that he had been aware of the cover-up shortly after the break-in occurred. August 9th on national TV, Richard Nixon announced to the country that he would resign the Presidency and was succeeded the following day by Vice President Gerald R. Ford. I was still assigned to Naval Air Station Kingsville, Tx. and I remember how shocked we all were at his announcement that evening on TV.

1976: July 4th The United States celebrates 200 years as a nation. I was on national TV, or shall I say along with several hundred others, I was in an audience of sailors all in our dress white uniforms. I was onboard the aircraft carrier U.S.S. Constellation homeported in San Diego, CA. The NBC network did a live simulcast from the flight deck of our ship and the deck of the old Frigate U.S.S. Constitution anchored in Boston harbor. Later someone in our family said they saw us on TV, because Cheryl was with me and it wasn't hard to see her green dress in a sea of white navy uniforms.

1980: Oregon, at 8:32 PDT on May 18th Mount St. Helens suddenly erupted with the force of 24 megatons of TNT ending a 123-year period of silent hibernation. The eruption column rose 80,000 feet (15 miles) into the air; grew to an estimated 40 miles in width and deposited its volcanic ash in 11 states. The eruption claims 57 lives and the entire north face of the mountain disappears in mere seconds. Damage estimates to the surrounding area is well over 2 billion dollars. I was stationed at Naval Air Station Kingsville, TX. again and most likely I was at work in the control tower or radar room.

1980: November 4th Ronald Reagan is elected as the 40th President of the United States. Reagan won the election over incumbent Jimmy Carter by a landslide, receiving the highest number of electoral votes (489) ever won by a non-incumbent presidential candidate. In 1984 as the incumbent candidate Reagan carried 525 electoral votes or 49 states against the Democrat Walter Mondale.

Ronald Wilson Reagan was born in Tampico, Illinois February 6, 1911. He grew up in several Illinois cities and graduated from Eureka College in 1932 after studying economics and sociology. The Reagan resume includes radio announcer for the Chicago Cubs; Movie Actor; TV show host; President of the Screen Actors Guild; Motivational Speaker for the General Electric Company; Product Spokesperson; Two Term Governor of California 1967-1975; Two Term President of the United States. It was during the Reagan presidency, we saw the end of the "Cold War" and the fall of the old Soviet Empire. Only 69 days into his first term on March 30, 1981 a would-be assassin shot President Reagan and three others in Washington. All survived.

Despite the continuing debate surrounding his legacy, many conservative and liberal scholars agree that Reagan has been the most influential president since Franklin D. Roosevelt. Sadly, in August 1994 at the age of 83 Reagan was diagnosed with Alzheimer's disease. Ten years later on June 5, 2004 President Reagan died at his home in Bel Air, CA. of pneumonia, complicated by Alzheimer's disease. A great leader is gone.

1986: On January 28th, the Space Shuttle Challenger lifted off at 11:39 AM with seven astronauts onboard. Then 73 seconds later all seven perished in a colossal explosion. The space program came to a very quick halt and President Reagan appointed a new commission to investigate the accident and determine the cause. I was stationed onboard the U.S.S. Guadalcanal, but myself and a friend were in Rome at the USO center near the Vatican when a USO volunteer gave us the news.

1989: November 9th the leader of the ruling East German Communist Party announced that citizens of the GDR could cross the border whenever they pleased. This marked the end of the "Berlin Wall." It was only two years earlier that President Ronald Reagan had called for the Russian leader to tear down the wall in his now famous speech near the Brandenburg Gate. During the walls 28-year history at least 171 men and women were killed, and more than 5,000 East Germans (including some 600 border guards) managed to cross the border to freedom.

I was stationed in Meridian, MS. and I remember sitting at home watching the news coverage as people began to climb all over the wall. Then they started to take hammers and picks to it and soon large portions of the wall began to fall as the crowds would yell and cheer. This was one of the highlights of the end of the "cold war" and the fall of the old Soviet Empire.

1995: April 19th a truck bomb exploded at 9:02 AM in front of the Alfred P. Murrah Federal Building in Oklahoma City. 168 men, women, and 19 children lost their lives. More than 650 other people were injured. A former army soldier, Timothy McVeigh was tried, convicted, and executed for the crime. At that very moment of the bombing I was on an airplane at the DFW Airport about to take off. We later learned what had happened and that the airport was closed because there had also been possible copycat threats against a federal building in Fort Worth and against an aircraft. We sat in the runway holding area for at least an hour before we could taxi back to the terminal.

2000: January 1st the new millennium and the "Millennium Bug" or Y2K bug as most referred to it. Do you remember either of the two movies called "The Day the Earth Stood Still?" Well this time it wasn't an alien invader from outer space, it was a computer software coding problem related to the date. It made the years 2000 and 1900 indistinguishable from each other, because software programs stored years with only two digits; for example, 1980 was stored as 80. So, when a computer date changed over to 2000 or "00" it would think the year was 1900 or would not recognize any year at all.

Because so many functions and aspects of our daily lives now depends on the use of computers, the Doomsday alarmist were predicting the total worldwide collapse of our society, Armageddon was at hand. You can see from the newspaper front page headlines all the things people were predicting to happen and all of the systems that would fail. Utility plants would fail thereby throwing the world into darkness and water supplies to our homes and business would dry up. Because so many of our vehicles have computer chips in them it's possible that transportation would come to a standstill.

I was working for Fujitsu North America and for over a year we had been working with our client accounts installing new program patches for this issue. We were so confident (really worried) that there would be no interruption of service that most of our agents and techs were either in their offices or at their customer sites until after midnight that evening. Just as midnight approached we held our breath waiting to see if anything happened….Nothing.

The computers remained on, all electrical power continued, and the phones remained silent, because it was the same with all our customers, no change. After a few minutes, we did start getting phone calls telling us all was well, with one exception, one of our own systems we forgot about in California. The company kept that little mistake quiet.

2001: September 11th, 2001 another date that will "live in infamy," the Twin Towers in New York City was the deadliest attack inside our borders ever, killing 2,977. Two airliners are flown into the towers killing 2,753 including 60 police officers and 343 firefighters. A third aircraft is flown into the Pentagon killing 184 including all 64 passengers aboard the aircraft. A fourth plane crashed in a field in Pennsylvania killing all 40 passengers and crew after several passengers subdued the hijackers. It's speculated that this fourth aircraft's intended target was most likely the U.S. Capital Building or even the White House.

I had been in the hospital and was in bed in our house in Saginaw, TX., still kind of weak and out of it. I remember Cheryl coming into our bedroom saying something like "David if you can get up your going to want to see this. They're attacking buildings in New York City." As I struggled to wake up I think I remember asking myself, "they" who is they? I was able to make it to the living room just in time to see the second aircraft fly into the second building, or it was a fast replay. I sat in my living room chair with my eyes glued to the TV and couldn't believe what was happening. This is America, something like this couldn't happen here. Well it did and it changed us all.

2003: February 1st, 8:59 AM EST the space shuttle Columbia disintegrated over Texas as it re-enters the earth's atmosphere. All 7 members of the crew were lost. It was determined that the cause came from protective tiles that were damaged during takeoff. The crew included 6 Americans and 1

Israeli. I don't remember where I was at the time it occurred, but when I got the news I remember thinking, was this the end of our shuttle program? Little did I know that all of our shuttles would soon be retired.

2005: April 2nd Pope John Paul II Dies and Benedict XVI is elected the next pope on April 24. John Paul II was the first Polish Pope and the third longest reigning Pope of 26 years.   The days of his last illness, lying in state, and his funeral drew millions to the Vatican. He was beatified in 2011. Now I'm not Catholic, but I was very interested in John Paul II having been honored to attend a Papal audience with him in 1986 when I was in Rome with a Navy friend. We would not agree on a lot of Biblical issues, but I had a lot of respect for him as a man and the life he lead.

2008: November 4th the 47-year-old Barack Obama defeats John McCain to become the 44th president and the first Black American President. The only thing we got from him was the government takeover of our country's health care system, "Obamacare."

2009: November 5th Major Nidal Hasan an Army Psychiatrist shoots and kills 13 and wounds dozens more at Fort Hood, TX. He is also shot and parylized. He is charged with 13 counts of murder and 32 counts of atempted murder.

2010: March 21st. The House of Representatives passes a bill that will overhaul (or destroy) the American health-care system. Proponents of the law spread the lie that the law will reduce the federal budget deficits by $143 billion over 10 years. It never did and costs are now rising.

2010: June 28th The Supreme Court rules 5-to-4 that the 2nd Amendment's guarantee, the right to keep and bear arms, applies too local and state gun control laws. Justice Samuel Alito, who spoke for the majority, said the right to self-defense is fundamental to American civil liberties.

2011: May 2nd U.S. special forces shoot and kill Osama bin Laden at last.

2012: September 11th Armed gunmen storm the American consulate in Benghazi, Libya, killing ambassador Christopher Stevens and three embassy officials. Questions still linger today on then State Department Secretary Hillary Clinton's and President Obama's involvement and foreknowledge of the attack.

2012: November 6th President Obama is stupidly re-elected. The American majority got **who** they voted for, but not **what** they voted for.

2013: On 11 February 2013, the Vatican confirmed that Pope Benedict XVI would resign the papacy because of his advanced age, becoming the first Pope to resign since Pope Gregory XII in 1415. The following month Jorge Mario Bergoglio, born December 17, 1936 in Buenos Aires, Argentina was elected Pope. He chose Francis as his papal name in honor of Saint Francis of Assisi.

2013: June 26th in a 5 to 4 vote the Supreme Court issues a ruling that the 1996 Defense of Marriage Act (DOMA) is unconstitutional and violates the rights of gays and lesbians. God save us.

2014: August 9th Ferguson, Mo. Police Officer Darren Wilson shoots and kills Michael Brown, an unarmed 18-year-old teenager. Details of the shooting are disputed. The next night protests turn violent. At a press conference, President Obama interferes and directs the Attorney General to "do what is necessary to help determine exactly what happened and to see that justice is done." Isn't that what the law does?

2014: November 24th A grand jury decides not to indict Officer Wilson. Protests erupt again even in other major cities. The whole mess was important to Cheryl and me, because our son Bryan is in St. Louis attending college just a mile or so from Ferguson. He also works campus security and was on duty the night that the grand jury decision was announced.

2015: June 26th The Supreme Court Rules in favor of Same-Sex Marriage. The Court rules that states cannot say that marriage is reserved for heterosexual couples. They may not be able to say it, but I can. Read your Bible don't just place your hand on it and swear to tell the truth.

2015: September 22nd Pope Francis arrives in Washington to begin his first visit to the United States. President Obama welcomes him at Andrews AFB. Pope Francis is the first pontiff ever to address a joint session of the U.S. Congress with over 500 lawmakers and guests. The speech addressed a broad range of issues affecting the country, including immigration, the death penalty and climate change.

2015: November 13th in three coordinated attacks terrorists kill 129 and wound hundreds more in Paris. Seven of the eight terrorists die during the attacks. The attacks are the worst violence in France since World War II. The French president calls the attack "an act of war," and retaliates with airstrikes on Raqqa, Syria, ISIS's self-declared capital.

2016: Where were you on August 4, 1972? I was getting married at 7:00 PM. Today August 4, 2016 Cheryl and I celebrate our 44th anniversary and boy have those years really gone by in a blink. We talked about several things we remembered over the years, but the funniest one was the fact we were having a very nice steak dinner tonight and 44 years ago, we couldn't hardly afford hot dogs or hamburger meat on the salary of a navy airman. They've been glorious years and now it's time to enjoy our retirement and our grandchildren.

2020: This will be the year forever known as the year of the worldwide pandemic COVID-19. Cases started showing up in 2019 in China where it's believed it originated. Soon the virus was showing up worldwide and there was no anti-virus shoot for it. Millions of cases were around the globe were diagnosed and tens of thousands were dying from complications brought on by the virus.

Many people that contract the virus only got sick like a bad case of the flu and soon recovered. I got it and it was not that bad on me, but two individuals I knew were not so lucky and passed away from the virus. The impact on the virus and all that federal and state governments required the population to do was devastating on the economy, business, families and individual lives.

- We were all required to self-quarantine if we had or thought we had come in contact with someone that was known to have the virus.
- We had to wear face masks wherever we left our homes.
- In public we were required to remain six feet apart from one another.
- Businesses were restricted as to the number or percentage of people at any one time.
- Many people worked from home if they had a job that could still be done in that manner, but so many people lost their jobs.
- Most restaurants went to take out or drive thru only in order to save their business.
- Hospitals were running out of beds for the sick and most non-life threating procedures were put on hold.
- Doctors were even doing appointments by video calls if it was for something already in your health record or something they didn't need to see you face to face for.

Now in May of 2021 Texas has ended the mask, the stay at home and other restrictions. We have fewer and fewer cases and life just might be returning to our pre-Covid time. Other states are following our example while liberals, the Democrats and others who have something to lose if there is no pandemic are outraged.

SECTION ELEVEN
STORIES FROM THE AIRPORT

Working any job at DFW Airport can be challenging and crazy but working for TSA and then DPS Airport Security has provided me with a book full of stories. These are all true stories because you just can't make this stuff up.

1. <u>**Is security effective**</u>? Before we get into the stories let's talk seriously about airport security. Almost every job I've held has involved physical or informational security in one way or another. From my navy career, which everything we did included some level of security, to being in computer tech support with Fujitsu North America; from TSA passenger screening to my employment with the Department of Public Safety, Airport Security Division at DFW International Airport.

Will we ever have a 100% secure transportation system for our airports, trains, buses, shipping and just as important now days, cyber-security. Well, the short answer is no, and the best we can ever hope for is to stay at least one step ahead of the bad guys. No matter what precautions you put in place someone will eventually find a way around them.

The following information is based on my time at DFW Airport. It seems like every day I was at work I heard someone complain about security procedures at the airport, but you let something happen and they'll be the first to say we aren't doing enough to protect the public.

The truth is they know they're not the bad guys, so they want the security just as long as it doesn't impact or inconvenience them, just everyone else. Any security is going to involve the loss of some freedom of movement, time, and privacy. At all airports we have a lot of security rules and regulations in place, but many of them are simply for show and do nothing to provide real security results.

At DFW Airport there were so many security holes when I worked there, I'm amazed that something has not already happened, and I pray that nothing ever does. The airport roadway system was designed and built for public convenience back in the 1970's and lets the public drive just about anywhere they want to go instead of channeling them to only the areas they need to go. Drivers can drive straight up to perimeter security gates that lead directly onto the aircraft ramp area or directly to the taxiway/runway areas.

The airport fuel storage tanks are next to a major roadway on the west side of the airport with only a regular chain link fence around it. The only security is one contract guard that sits inside the main building and operates the main entrance gate remotely.

Depending on whose numbers you read this is the approximate size of the airport. Manhattan Island, New York is 22.7 square miles, DFW Airport is 27 square miles (17,500 acres) with over 37 miles of airfield perimeter fence line, much of which is unmonitored most of the time. There are remote areas where it would not be hard at all for someone to get through or over the 6 ft. fence undetected.

The dumbest thing I think is we allowed curbside parking at all terminals. If you want a big headline a person can come from anywhere, drive through one of two toll plazas and right up to any terminal or hangar facility and park a vehicle of any type or size within 25 feet of a main entrance door and never be stopped or checked in any way.

They let delivery vans, buses, taxicabs, and limousines park wherever they want to next to the terminal curbs. HELLO, anyone out there remember the federal building in Oklahoma City or the first attack on the New York City Twin Towers basement! Both of those were vans.

The local media has aired several stories about terminal parking and unattended vehicles, but officials tell the public that there's no problem at the airport, but they're only blowing smoke. What they don't tell you is that we were very understaffed in both the police and security divisions but, we added more foot and vehicle patrols in the terminals and the parking garages.

What the airport needs to do is adopt a serious attitude about cleaning up the traffic and parking problems at the terminals. Until they change the traffic and parking regulations there'll continue to be a very serious issue and very real danger to the public and airport employees.

According to MercuryNews.com and several other articles TSA had a 95% failure rate at finding test weapons at the checkpoints due to poor training and equipment.[58] Also, they continue to have a high turnover rate of employees. When I left TSA, it was a turnover rate of 22% at DFW Airport and according to The American Federation of Government Employees (AFGE) the following information was provided on their website:

"It's no secret that TSA is one of the worst places to work – years of employee satisfaction surveys have shown that TSA officers' morale is constantly the lowest or among the lowest in the federal government.

As a union representing TSA officers, we know exactly why. Years of TSA's resistance to our union's repeated calls to improve working conditions and follow the same rules as other Homeland Security components have made the agency among the worst places to work in the government.

TSA is resisting our calls to make the agency a better place to work because it believes it can do whatever it wants under the law creating TSA that gave the agency wide discretion on personnel issues. That's why people are leaving, and new numbers recently obtained through a Freedom of Information Act request by Bloomberg Law showed how bad the situation is.

Among the 10 major airports in the U.S., TSA hired 8,553 officers between 2012 and 2016, but nearly as many – 7,784 officers – left the agency during the same time period. While federal employees' overall turnover rate registered at about 15%, TSA officers' turnover rate at those airports ranged between 30% and 80%."

The 4 reasons cited by the American Federation of Government Employees (AFGE) as to why officers are leaving in droves are: "1) Low Pay with the average office making around $37,000 per year. 2) Dangerous Job facing possible terrorists, explosives, disgruntled travelers who either verbally abuse the officers or even physically attack them. 3) Few workplace rights. This is a big one in my opinion. Even though TSA officers are federal employees, they don't have the same rights as other employees at other agencies, thanks to the law creating TSA that gave the agency wide discretion on what it wants to do with employees.

TSA officers, for example, do not have statutory Family and Medical Leave Act (FMLA) protections. As a result, many TSA officers are penalized for taking unpaid time off to take care of themselves or their ill family members. TSA fires people simply because they have an illness or condition—not because it effects how well they do their jobs.

This is a violation of the Rehabilitation Act elsewhere in the government. TSA officers do not have the right to appeal adverse decisions to the independent Merits Systems Protection Board, which means TSA is the judge, jury, and executioner on its own decisions. TSA officers also fear retaliation for raising complaints, including for filing charges with the Equal Employment Opportunity Commission. Surprisingly, TSA managers have more workplace rights than frontline TSA officers do." [59]

Airline and other company employees are able to park their vehicles in the employee parking lots, be picked up by a company vehicle, drive up to a security gate and enter the aircraft ramp area and never be checked as to what they might be carrying on their person or in their lunch boxes and back packs. The procedures by DPS security personnel are to verify that the vehicle has a current airport sticker, make a visual check of the vehicle contents, and electronically scan all occupant's airport badges to ensure they are authorized to enter the ramp at that location.

Only at rare times is a full check of the vehicle conducted, but the occupants never undergo a scan or physical pat down. The only exception to this is certain venders delivering at one gate during a specific time frame. So, the point is that a person can without any difficultly take weapons or drugs right through security and right out onto the airport security areas without ever being challenged or searched.

Once inside the ramp area employees are able to go anywhere they want, jet bridges, airplanes, baggage areas, airline workspaces and offices or enter the terminals from dozens of employee entries, all without being screened. I'm in the terminals every day and I see ramp personnel all over the place. Sitting in gate lounge areas, in stores and restaurants and they have more freedom of movement than security personnel do.

To make this even worse we had two man teams called Internal Threat Teams (ITT) that go to random locations in the terminals and check employees as they enter the secure side from the ramp area. The idea is that we can catch employees with prohibited items. The problem is that when I ask you to empty your pockets or show me what is in your backpack, you show me only what you want too and leave the prohibited item hidden.

I'm not allowed to pat you down or use a metal detector wand to verify nothing was left in your pockets and the same applies to any bag you are carrying. So, I've accomplished absolutely nothing. The employees aren't stupid, because the word gets out very quick where we are, so they just use a different door 100 ft. away to enter the terminal.

We allow anyone to be signed in and escorted with proper ID to go out on the ramp areas where the aircraft are located. We have absolutely no idea who these people are, let alone what their backgrounds are. Gates are provided a list of individuals that are not allowed to enter for various reasons, but most gate officers will not even look at them.

Most of workers entering are temporary day workers with a contractor and I will venture to say that a good percentage of them are illegal aliens from south of the border. We have had no training on official forms of identification. Someone could hand us a fake passport, or a forged consulate card and chances are we would never know it. The contractors are happy with this arrangement, because they don't have to spend the money to get them an airport identification badge.

The terrible truth about security at our nations' airports is that a lot of what we do is said to be a deterrent, but it's just for show and results in no tangible security measures. The way we are told to perform a lot of our procedures can be circumvented and are a complete waste of time, money, and manpower, but supervision and management will not listen or accept any input from the officers, it's seen as a challenge to their leadership and authority.

Do we get lucky sometimes and catch something, of course we do, but even a blind dog gets lucky and finds a bone sometimes? It's more important that we appease TSA Inspectors and put on a face that plays good to the public and the media. There is no doubt that another tragedy is going to happen, I just pray it's not here at DFW Airport.

2. <u>In the beginning</u>. I was one of the originals with TSA at DFW Airport. I started in Terminal C working both checked baggage and passenger screening and then moved to Terminal E where I stayed with passenger screening the rest of my time. As soon as Terminal D's construction was completed I was with a crew that opened it up and worked checkpoint D18 until I resigned. I was with TSA a total of 3 ½ years.

When we first started we still had law enforcement officers assigned to each checkpoint. I remember on several occasions reporting to my checkpoint only to find that the "threat level" had been increased and all the law enforcement officers were in full riot gear including automatic rifles. That wasn't always a comforting feeling. Our own airport police were going through a lot of changes and ramping up to take over all law enforcement activities after about a year.

3. **<u>This is a test</u>**! After we had been there just over a year the agency started testing us at random times and locations to see if we were doing things correctly. One day a man was walking through the metal detector it alarmed, so he was sent back because he had a cell phone still clipped on his waistband. As he came through a second time he still alarmed so he was sent to me for a hand wand and pat down.

I explained what I was going to do and proceeded with the hand wand. When I got to his waistband the wand sounded so I had to do a pat down with my hand. When I did, I put my thumb right on the hammer of a gun hidden inside the waistband. We were toe to toe and without moving any further, I looked him in the eyes and told him don't move, then I yelled for the supervisor. Now of course I'm giving this guy my most fearsome look and he is terrified at what I might do if he moves. Sure he was, what was really going on is I'm about to wet my pants, because at that moment I don't know if this is real or not and could this guy be a nut case that is about to shoot us all.

The supervisor hit the "panic button" to call the police and to start the checkpoint cameras and voice recorders. This guy now declared himself to be a TSA inspector and the weapon was only a training device. I had passed the test, but before my heart rate came down too normal I still wanted to smack this guy for putting me and everyone else through this panic drill.

4. **<u>The dearly departed</u>**. Ok, how about one on the lighter side. One day I was up front helping people put their belongings on the belt to go through the x-ray machine when this lady steps up and hands me a small container and a piece of paper. When I asked her what the container was

she replied, "That's my husband." I'm sure the look on my face was priceless, because I had not yet had anyone bring the ashes of their loved one through the checkpoint.

The supervisor came over and schooled me on the screening of human ashes at airports. Well, we put George or whatever his name might have been through the x-ray and the lady was on her way. If this was one they covered in training they didn't spend enough time on it.

5. <u>Surprise</u>! At first, we were also doing random gate checks, which were a waste of time. They would send a male and a female team to a gate just as travelers were lining up to board the plane. We would randomly select individuals in line and recheck their carryon baggage and hand wand them. The idea is to catch any prohibited items that might have been missed here or where they came from if they were making a connecting flight.

So, on this day we pulled a female out of line. Anytime you hand wand someone or perform a pat down it has to be same gender. So, I took the ID and carry-on baggage to a table as my partner began to hand wand the individual. I completed my bag inspection and then picked up the ID and looked at it, then as I turned around I noticed that this was an ID for a male and this male was a doctor.

I quickly looked at the person and everything I saw said female until you got up close. I didn't say a thing to my partner until after the individual had gotten back in line, then I told her what had happened. She stated that she thought there was something "very different about that female," but continued to wand the person anyway.

On another occasion a flight for New York was just about loaded when a guy came running up at the last second. Now there was an unwritten rule that the last person on was checked so the gate agent directed him over to my partner. The man was mad when he kicked off his shoes, removed his belt and then asked if I wanted his pants. Well, Mr. Smart mouth didn't notice the 6'4" police officer that was standing over by the gate counter watching his little tantrum. I just looked over at the officer and he came over and stood next to the man that was only about 5'6".

The officer said something like "we need to change our attitude, don't we?" The short little New Yorker still wanted to argue with the officer, but the Police Officer wasn't having any of his foolishness. He asked for the man's ID and then stepped aside to run a check on him over the radio with dispatch.

My partner and I waited patiently and then after a couple of minutes we watched as the officer towered over him and very sternly told him how things are done down here in Texas and when the man came back to me he was very humble and cooperative. He made his flight to New York as he was last seen galloping down the jet bridge with his shoes in one hand and his laptop bag bouncing over his shoulder.

6. <u>And the winner is!</u> On evening we had a young man come through the checkpoint with a small roller bag that only had a couple of items in it, but one of the items created a very large solid image on the x-ray. Well of course the TSA operator called for a bag check and when it was opened there was a beautiful motion picture "Oscar" award. It had belonged to the man's father who had just passed away and he explained that his father was a writer in the early days of movies. I'm sure he told us what movie he had won it for, but I don't remember now.

TSA was still young and still developing, not just the rules, but the TSA personnel also. We had a young female lead on duty and she immediately started telling the man that he could not take "Oscar" onboard in his carry-on luggage because it was heavy and could be used as a weapon. We looked at her and basically said you're crazy, we're not doing this to this man that just lost his father. One of us put the award back in the bag and sent him on his way. The inexperienced Lead didn't want to challenge us, so she let it go.

7. <u>Pull your pants up</u>! There was a whole family coming through the checkpoint one day and a teenage boy about 15 or 16 years old had to be wanded because he made the walkthrough scanner alarm, so he was sent to me. The young boy had on baggy pants that were really sagging because he didn't have a belt on. You all know that when you hand wand someone you just follow the outline of the person all the way around including on the inside of the legs and up passed the inner thigh. Well you get the picture.

I told this youngster to pull his pants up, but he only responded with a sigh. Then with his parents watching I got up close and personal, held the round wand up in front of face and told him "son you better pull those pants up as far as you can, because I'm going all the way home with this wand, do you understand?" With a very different look on his face I got immediate cooperation from him and an approving look from his father.

8. <u>What's in your pocket</u>? In a similar situation I was hand wanding a young man while his family was getting their things together and waiting on him. When my wand went by one of his jean pockets it would alarm, so I instructed him to make sure he had everything removed from his pockets. He pulled out something and laid it aside, but my wand continued to alarm.

When I told him to turn his pocket inside out he leaned forward and whispered to me that he had a condom in a foil package in his pocket and please don't make him take it out in front of his family. Sorry kid, I had to do it and the look on his parent's faces was not good. His sister on the other hand was enjoying every second knowing what would most likely happen later.

9. <u>We have a security breach.</u> This very serious anywhere, but at an airport it could cost lives and/or millions of dollars to an airline operation and the airport no matter whether it's a person or a piece of luggage. On three occasions I was on duty when we had a breach and had to empty the terminals searching for someone who may have gotten through security without being properly checked. The one I remember most, I was working in Terminal C and because of the time between the suspected breach and the notification, the individual could have been anywhere.

So they had to empty and search three of the four connected terminals. There was no Terminal D yet. TSA and the police emptied all passengers, airline employees, store employees, cleaning personnel, customer service personnel and terminal management to the street side of the terminals.

Then we went store by store, office by office and toilet by toilet searching for this person. At the same time the personnel that monitored the close circuit TV cameras were reviewing their tapes and checking to see where he might have gone. It seemed like it would take forever to search a whole terminal, after all on the secured side each terminal was slightly over three quarters of a mile long.

They never found the person and after about thirty or forty minutes the search was ended and now it was time to rescreen an estimated three thousand people back into the terminals. Man was there some irate folks. At first we screened only airline personnel, because nobody was going anywhere until the flight crews and the gate agents were there to check the passengers in and the flight crews to get the airplanes ready. Next were the store employees and terminal management, because the stores and restaurants had been left open and unattended.

Finally, the passengers, and man there sure were a lot of them that just couldn't understand why they all had to leave the terminal while we searched and then of course they didn't understand why they had to be the last ones' to be allowed back in. That was a very long day, one that we never wanted to repeat again.

10. <u>Personalities in full public view</u>. If you work long enough at a public place like an airport eventually you're bound to see or meet someone of notoriety. One evening a young lady came up to the checkpoint placing all her property in an x-ray bin and then walked through the metal detector. She alarmed and was told to step back and remove her shoes. It was about this time I was walking around the machine taking some of the bins back up front.

The lady had already taken her belt off so as she bent over to remove her shoes her denim pants began to fall and as I turned around I got an eye full! A few minutes later the x-ray operator who had seen all this happen asked me with some excitement in his voice if I knew who that was, to which I stated no. He informed me that I had just been mooned by a young singer and actress Hillary Duff. Ms. Duff had also had a few drinks before coming to the airport. I was not impressed with her or her "derriere."

Another evening I was on a break and had gone into a nearby coffee shop. There was just me and one other customer in the store when I noticed a man sitting at a nearby table signing 8"x10" photo's. It was actor Martin Sheen, who at that time was the star of the television show "The West Wing." He asked me if I would like to have one and of course I said yes. At the time, Cheryl and I were big fans of the show in which he played the role of president.

It was between seasons and when it came back on we would learn if he had been re-elected or not. As he handed me the photo I greeted him with a handshake and asked him if he could give me a little hint as to the opening episode of the new season, but he only smiled and said he was sworn to secrecy.

I also met country singer Ronnie Dunn of "Brooks & Dunn" one day at the food court in Terminal C. He wasn't in the mood to sing. Danny Glover from the movie "Lethal Weapon" came through one night and he had to go through a pat down. He was not very happy about it and thought we were a bunch of government workers that couldn't get a real job. I have also met or seen several sports figures and elected officials, but you know what, they're all just travelers when it comes to security and they all must comply with the same set of rules whether they like it or not.

11. <u>ENOUGH</u>! After about three years a lot of us had had just about enough of "the good ole boys" and the things that were going on in TSA. Around the spring of 2006 TSA had about a 22% turnover rate nationwide and I believe it may have even been higher than that at DFW airport. It was in early April and I had just had a medical procedure done, and when I came back I was able to do everything except my doctor didn't want me lifting anything heavy for a week, such as passenger luggage.

So I turned in a request to my supervisor for light duty and was told it would have to go over to headquarters and it would take a couple of days. Well I said ok I could take a couple of sick days, but a couple turn into a week and then two weeks. I had checked just about every day with my supervisor and the office, but I keep getting the run around with no answers. Then finally I found out that the screening manager had not even turned in my request and I had waisted twelve days of sick time.

One day at work something happened that just set me off. I had had enough of TSA and I left the checkpoint and went down to the manager's office and threw my badge on his desk while proclaiming "you need me more than I need you" and then I walked out. The next day I put all my uniforms in a large black trash bag, drove over to the Federal Security Directors/TSA headquarters in Coppell, walked into the office of the lady that does your exit paperwork and interviews. To her amazement I dropped that trash bag in the middle of her office floor.

I proceeded to tell her what I was doing, that the terminal manager had my badge and asked what papers she needed me to sign. With a puzzled looked on her face she stated that you have to make an appointment. I stopped her in mid-sentence and stated that no I didn't, that this was the only time I was coming there and that whatever she needed, it had better get done right now because I was not ever coming back. We took care of everything and I never returned.

One year later I got a check in the mail from TSA. I pulled out my last statement from them to see what my rate of pay was and sure enough the check was equal to twelve days of pay. I was already working for the Airport Department of Public Safety and I found out that the TSA security manager I had given my badge to had been fired and was up on possible rape charges on a female TSA agent.

I guessed that for some reason Washington must have audited everything he did and in my case, he was wrong and decided to pay me for those twelve days. I gladly cashed the check. I'm very sorry for whoever that young lady was, but for me I guess there was a little bit of justice.

12. <u>**Dallas/Fort Worth International Airport**</u>. Advance forward to when I was working at DFW International Airport, Security Division which is a part of the Department of Public Safety. All the following information was current as of August 2016.

This airport is one of the most unique, complex, and largest airports in the world. DFW is the 5th busiest airport in the world (in terms of aircraft operations) and ranks 15th in terms of passenger movements at the time of this writing. There are 23 passenger airlines, 10 domestic and 13 foreign. It is a major 24-hour shipping hub for FedEx, UPS, and DHL. There are also cargo shipping companies from all over the world.

Airport Specifics:

- 17,207 acres or 27 square miles. More land mass than Manhattan Island.

- 7 Runways with a spider web of taxiways and roadways.

- 5 separate terminals with a 6th planned in 2022 or 2023.

• Built between Dallas and Fort Worth on land from 4 cities it has its own infrastructure like any large city with its own postal zip code and city designation "DWF Airport, TX. 75261.

• The CEO is the mayor, and the executive board of directors is the city council.

• Just like any city government structure, they have their own power plant, water collection/treatment plant, street and city maintenance department. Their own aircraft fuel depot and vehicle gas stations. Convenience stores, all major rental car companies and even a pet boarding company are located on airport.

• Within DPS is the police department, fire department, Medical/EMS, and airport security. They operate their own 911 emergency dispatch center. There is jail facility on airport, and they staff their own SWAT, EOD/K-9 Teams, and a Criminal Investigations Division.

• There are six fire stations fully staffed at all times that provide fire protection for the entire airport, aircraft operations, and all businesses on airport property and mutual aid agreements with surrounding cities. A Fire Training Academy that trains fire fighters from all over the world in advanced techniques of aircraft fires and rescue.

• EMS operates four critical care ambulances from the airport to three local hospitals and two Level 1 trauma centers. If required, "Care Flight" helo's can be on site in a matter of minutes.

• There is a group of people tucked away in one building just watching all of the hundreds of cameras that are used in airport surveillance. They are recording all activities throughout all the terminals, aircraft ramps and operating areas, parking lots and the main roadways 24/7. "Big Brother" is watching.

• They have a Health & Wellness Center with gym facilities for airport and airline employees. There is a full service 18-hole golf course that is open to the general public.

• The airport operates it's on bus system and an elevated bi-directional train on a scenic 4.9-mile track that connects all five terminals. Two fast rail systems connect the airport with downtown Dallas and Fort Worth.

• Hyatt Hotels operates three major hotels on airport property.

Within my first year of working at DPS I had qualified and worked in all of our assignments and helping others wherever I could. I made an impression on someone because at the end of that first year I was selected as DFW Airport DPS New Employee of the Year. I received a large trophy, a uniform medal, a handshake and then told to go back to work. Now that I've told you the boring facts about the airport and my first award let's look at some stories.

13. **<u>Do I appear drunk</u>**? I was on terminal duty and had just walked out to make a patrol walk of the upper curb area. A lady I guess to be in her mid-thirties was sitting on a bench and she asked me how to get to the rental car center. I explained to her that she needed to go down to the lower level and catch a bus to the Rental Car Center located on the south end of the airport. She went and sat back down to finish her cigarette and a minute or so later she walked back up to me and looking directly into my face asked, "in your professional opinion sir do I appear drunk?"

Considering that I'm in a dark blue uniform with DPS patches on my sleeves and a shield above my pocket, a portable radio, and she's asking me this question, now I'm slow sometimes, but it didn't take me long to figure out she's had too many drinks. She is close enough to my face that her breath was also a dead giveaway. Shame on me for letting her get that close to me. I asked her if she had any mints or gum and then politely told her that in my "professional opinion" she should forget the rental car and I directed her to a nearby cab stand. She was glad to comply.

14. <u>Don't make a female officer mad</u>. One night I was working the overnight shift when we heard a radio call go out for a hit and run accident with injuries at the south Toll Plaza. You hear all the police units check in and then a fire truck and an ambulance. I was on vehicle patrol so I started down that direction, because sometimes the police will use us for traffic control or other duties.

After the first police unit driven by one of our female officers arrives on scene we find out what really happened. There was a young couple that as they pulled up to the Toll Plaza the male driver failed to stop and ran into the backend of the vehicle in front of them. The driver was intoxicated, he panicked, exited the vehicle, and started running, leaving his pregnant "girlfriend" in the vehicle. The next thing we hear on the radio is the female officer reporting she is in foot pursuit. Where he thought he was going to run to no one knows. Other arriving officers attend to the girlfriend and the occupants of the other vehicle.

It was not too hard for the officer to catch up with the intoxicated driver and forcefully put his face in the pavement while cuffing his hands behind his back. For the next couple of days everyone in DPS was talking about the next radio call from the female officer and how slightly out of breath she was, but mostly how really mad she was and how you could clearly hear the anger in her voice.

I would not have wanted to be that guy when that officer body slammed him down on the concrete roadway, put her knee in his back and then twisted his arms around his back. To say nothing about how this piece of trash abandoned that young women after an accident. Now what made her mad the most, the fact that she had to chase him down or that he left his pregnant girlfriend. No matter, his next ride that night was to jail and not at the airport, he got to see the Dallas County Jail.

15. **Stupid questions**. If you're a traveler and you have a question then you're going to ask someone who works at the airport. A police or security officer walking around the terminal is the ideal person to ask, so we get a lot of questions and requests such as:

Traveler: Can you tell me where the nearest restroom is?

Officer: Look behind you!

Traveler: [While standing 10 ft. from an exit]: Sir, can you tell me where the closest exit is?

Officer: Yes Ma'am, all the way down by gate 31.

Random security checks at the departure gate during boarding.

Traveler: [Elderly lady] You only pulled me out of line because I'm Jewish!

Officer: No Ma'am, my mistake, today it's Presbyterians.

A couple pulls up to a restricted vehicle access security gate.

Driver: I think we're lost, we've been driving around in circles for over 45 minutes.

Officer: I think that's a new record!

Young woman pulls up in her fancy sports car to a restricted vehicle security
gate where she shouldn't be.

Driver: The road signs aren't clear, [They state no public access] how do I get to the Hyatt Hotel.

Officer: You can't get there from here. You have to go home and start all over again.

Driver: Facial expression becomes one of fear and confusion, until the officer smiles. You've got to have some fun sometimes.

Two ladies pull up to terminal curbside in front of a security officer.

Passenger: Sir, we're lost and trying to find the interstate to Oklahoma City.

Officer: Ma'am you missed the interstate by about 10 miles to the east, but I think we have a flight leaving within the hour.

At a TSA Terminal Checkpoint.

Traveler: Why are you people bothering innocent travelers instead of looking for the real terrorists?

Officer: Sir, please describe to me what a real terrorist looks like or just point one out to me?

At a TSA Terminal Checkpoint.

Traveler: Two young loudmouth men approach the x-ray machine and as they begin to load their items on the belt one guy in a loud tone asked, Have you found any bombs today!

Everyone: It was like someone paused the movie and you could have heard a pin drop.

16. **<u>You can't park there</u>**. One of our duties in the terminals is to make sure, for safety and security reasons, there are no unattended vehicles left at the curb and to help the police and the parking folks with parking and traffic problems. One evening I stepped out front to walk the curb and a female driver was double parked right in front of an entrance and blocking the Terminal-Link bus and the taxicab stand. I approached the vehicle on the driver's side and ask the lady to please move her vehicle, to which she replied, "I'm waiting for someone to come out and you don't have the authority to tell me where I can park." On any other day, I would have just smiled and politely told her the parking regulation.

Immediately my anger rose up and I informed the lady she didn't want to go there with that attitude, and she was about to find out in a sudden and dramatic way what kind of authority I had as I reached for the microphone on my DPS radio. I informed her that if necessary I could have as many police officers on scene as I needed in about sixty seconds. Quickly she changed her stubborn attitude and drove away.

On another occasion, almost the same thing happened, I walked out, and a man pulled up, blocking the bus stop. I informed him he could not park there and needed to move his vehicle to one of the designated passenger pickup areas. He responded telling me he was waiting for someone to come out and he didn't want to move from his spot. I asked him one more time to which he had some less than appropriate language, so as I'm reaching for my ticket book and my radio I told him, "Sir that's ok, it's best that your car isn't moving while I'm writing this ticket and calling it in to police dispatch for a tow truck." Immediately his window went up as he drove away.

17. <u>Child endangerment</u>. One hot day I walked up on a car that had no one in the front seat and I notice at least two small children in the rear seat. My anger (and not my Christian attitude) was immediately on display and as I reached for my radio to call dispatch the owner of the car came running up yelling "this is my car sir." With all the force, I could muster I began to lecture him about leaving his car unattended, but much more important was the small children left in the vehicle by themselves.

After hearing what I had to say about the dangers of leaving his children in the car, this fool still wanted to give me a bunch of lame excuses. I told him I didn't want to hear them and then I instructed him to get in his car and leave before I had him arrested for child endangerment. With that statement I got his full attention and he proceeded to drive away. I stayed in the area for a while just to make sure he didn't return and do it again. I pray he never does that again with those children.

18. <u>Room service not included</u>. I'm standing at the top of an escalator that comes up from an underground tunnel and I'm just watching people and answering questions for travelers as they come by. All of a sudden a young lady came off of the escalator proclaiming that a man was down below urinating in a corner and appeared to be drunk. I told her I would take care of it, but before I got too far from my location a young man walked up to me and in slightly slurred speech asked me where he could smoke a cigarette. I told him he had to go outside, and I would be glad to show him where.

As I lead him through the exit he was trying to tell me how this was his first time to fly and that he had drank a few beers and taken some medication. Well no wonder he thought the corner was a good place to, you know. He continued asking me if I was going to show him how to get back to his gate after he finished his cigarette. I assured him that I was going to take good care of him.

As he was enjoying his cigarette out on the curb I was on my radio calling for a police response to my location and in less than a minute I had an officer with me and a patrol car pulling up. After the police asked him a few questions he was gently loaded into the patrol car and was booked into a 6'x 8' room free of charge for the night in the airport jail. Room service not included.

19. <u>He kidnaped my son</u>! On another occasion I'm standing at the platform where the Terminal Link trains run when a lady with a small child in a stroller comes running up to me declaring that someone has kidnaped her other son. It takes a few minutes to get her to stop crying so I can understand what she's saying. Apparently she had just arrived from New York and as she got off the airplane her ex-husband was there to greet them. Somehow he walked off with the older boy and onto a train to another terminal.

Knowing this could be a case of parental kidnapping I wanted to act fast and do the right thing. I had just seen a Police Officer down the escalator in the main terminal, so I told the lady to follow me. We got in the elevator and thankfully the officer was still there when we arrived. I informed him what was going on and we immediately contacted dispatch and put in motion procedures to locate the husband and the boy. The lady told us that her ex-husband now lives in Southern California so we checked the boards for flights he could be on and a few minutes later he and the boy were found in another terminal about to board a flight to Orange County, California.

Officers in that terminal interviewed him and found out that he had joint custody of the boy and had the court paperwork to verify it, so it was determined that he could leave with the boy. Then officers found out that the lady worked for child protective services here in the local area and was just trying to manipulate the situation against him. I think the lady had some more questions to answer.

20. <u>Get Off That Fence</u>. One sunny day I had just arrived at my assigned airfield gate for the day and relieved a young female officer. I had just cleared a vehicle through my gate, and I noticed a woman walking up the access roadway when she stopped about 30 feet away from me and reached out to pull herself up on the security fence. I immediately approached her and told her to get off the security fence and asked why she was trying to climb it. She was a young lady in her early 30's and she responded that she was going to get her car, to which I replied that her car was not in there, this is a ramp area where the airplanes park. As she was hanging on the fence by her legs she turned her face to me and asked, "then where is my car!"

As I continued to try to talk to this woman, the officer I had just relieved was about to drive off but saw what was going on and pulled her car up to the gate and used her cell phone to call airport 911. This lady was obviously disturbed, off her medication or something and now she put her left leg between the top of the fence and the row of razor wire just above it. I'm not touching the women or helping her in any way and as I demanded she come down she pulled her leg back and came down and stood next to the fence. She was wearing denim shorts and as I looked down at her leg she had ripped it open on the razor wire and had blood running down her leg. The cut was so deep I could see muscle fiber in the wound.

I continued to talk to her asking her to step away from the security fence and pleading with her to look down at her leg. She never once looked down, she just stood there and stared at me. I realized that she had no idea that she was injured and when I stood three feet from her and looked her in the eyes it was just a blank empty almost lifeless expression. It also went through my mind that she could be having some kind of psychotic episode and I could be in physical danger.

The whole event only lasted about five minutes. In less than a couple of minutes I had several police cars, an ambulance and security supervisors all on scene with me and I was very glad to let them take over. As a female police officer was trying to talk to her and get some information a paramedic was spraying something on her leg wound. I know that would have stung like crazy, but that woman didn't even know he was doing it. She was still asking where her car was and now as officers and paramedics were trying to get her on the stretcher and into the ambulance she decides to become combative. It took about five people to subdue her and finally handcuff and strap her down on the stretcher. She was immediately taken to Parkland Hospital in Dallas.

21. <u>**This Is An Exercise**</u>. One day before I got ready for work I received a phone call from my assistant security manager asking if I would like to participate in a training exercise with the Police EOD/K-9 unit. Of course, I said yes and left for work about two hours early. Arriving at Terminal C, I parked my truck and met up with one of the K-9 officers in the parking garage.

The officer explained he would be the exercise control officer, what the exercise was all about and what he wanted me to do. Then he gave me a small piece of rolling carry-on luggage and I knew there had to be something like drugs or explosive material in it, but I didn't even want to ask. When the officer left I suddenly felt a little strange. It was a controlled exercise, and I knew I was okay, but still I was walking around with something that was illegal and it had to be real, or the exercise wouldn't work.

The control officer needed time to get all the other players in place, so I walked around the parking garage for a while just killing time. About twenty minutes later the control officer called me on my cell phone telling me that everyone was in place for the exercise, so I proceeded to one of the terminal entrances with my new piece of luggage. As I entered the terminal building I was near a baggage claim area so there was a lot of people and other luggage moving about in different directions.

Dressed in blue jeans, a button down collar shirt, a ball cap and sneakers I stood in the entrance for a few seconds looking in all directions to see where the other players were. I saw the K-9 Officer, the dog and the control officer who had positioned himself further down the hallway. A couple of flights must have just come in because there was a lot of travelers claiming their luggage and moving about. As I started walking down the hallway with other travelers and their luggage going in both directions, I was hoping to walk right by the K-9 officer and her dog that were about 25 yards ahead of me.

The object of the exercise was to test the K-9 dog in a very fluid moving environment, to see if the dog got a hit on a substance. Then determine which moving bag was it in and could the K-9 then keep up with it regardless of what direction it was moving among all the other people and luggage. You know how chaotic it can get around a baggage claim area sometimes. Whatever I was carrying in that bag it wasn't hard for this super K-9 to nail the bag I was dragging behind me!

As I walked by, the dog immediately alerted on my bag and I felt him nudge it with his nose. Now remember I'm playing a role and only one person knows who I really am. These people know they are being tested, but at this point they have no idea if this is the test or do they have a real world situation.

In my immediate area is the K-9 dog and his handler, a very tall and somewhat masculine female police officer, a SWAT officer in full gear, a terminal police officer, and my control officer who was running the exercise. I was soon to discover there was also a plain clothes detective from the airport Criminal Investigation Division (CID). I have met the SWAT officer from a previous ride-out when I was helping in the 911 dispatch office, so I was trying to avoid facing his direction or making any eye contact with him or any of the others.

When I felt the dog nudge my bag I turned around and looked back at the K-9 officer and asked her if there was a problem, to which she replied "no sir" so I turned and continued on. Now most of the time these dogs are alerting on objects that are stationary like in a vehicle or a container in a warehouse so when they get a hit the dog will sit next to the suspect or suspect item and that is the signal. In this case the dog sat down, but I kept walking so of course the luggage moved away from the K-9, so the dog was somewhat confused as to what he was supposed to do. Now I knew I had been detected by the dog, but I needed to play out the scenario so when the dog nudged my luggage a second time I stopped and became a little indignant with the K-9 officer.

It was now that the plain clothes officer came out of nowhere, stepped up to me, displayed his badge and asked me to leave my bag where it was and step aside for a few questions. I had no idea how long the exercise would go on so now I started acting like I was a little confused as to what was going on. As we stepped off to the side of the hall the officer asked me for some identification. I nervously gave him my driver's license trying not to let him see my airport DPS ID that was right behind my license in my wallet. Dummy me I forgot to take it out or hide it. I also asked him what was going on, why did you stop me? Now I'm looking at all of the other officers as the K-9 officer is looking my bag over and about to open it up.

The plain clothes officer being a detective began asking me probing questions trying to find out who I really was, where I came from and where I was going. What flight I was on, where was my ticket and why was I taking the flight. I was taken back by all of this questioning and so I started making up one heck of a story and I thought I was doing pretty good, but as we progressed I was starting to run out of answers for this officer and my story was starting to fall apart. Just like it would in a real world situation I guess.

I told him I was working for one of the contract companies at the airport and that I had a one-day meeting in Chicago I was flying up for. When he asked me for my ticket and what flight I was on all I could think to tell him was it was in my bag. In the meantime, the other officers had opened the luggage and discovered what was in it and it was about this time I think the detective was about to slap the handcuffs on me. Remember only one officer knows if this is an exercise or am I the real deal so everyone is proceeding as if they had just made a real drug bust.

I believe I was about to find myself face down in the middle of the baggage claim area with my hands behind my back. Thankfully it was at this point the control officer stepped in and informed everyone this was an exercise, and I was saved from an embarrassing moment of being placed under arrest in front of a huge public crowd.

We all stepped off to one side away from the public and did a little debrief right there. The only input I had was that the whole time I was being questioned I was standing there facing my bag with my cell phone in my hand nervously rolling it around. I told the detective that I believe he should have taken it away from me or asked me to put it away. The reason being that the bag could have contained a bomb instead of drugs and the phone itself could have been the trigger.

The SWAT officer agreed and stated he himself should have picked up on that right away. He also stated that for officer safety they should have put me in handcuffs from the beginning. I was rather glad they didn't. It was fun, but now that they all know me it would be hard to pull off a similar exercise again with me in it.

22. **<u>Airport 911 What's The Location Of Your Emergency</u>**? Because they were understaffed I worked at the airport DPS Dispatch office taking 911 calls for a little over a year. I was told I was chosen, because I had been an air traffic controller and knew how to deal with stressful situations. I didn't tell them there is a big difference in the type of stress they were talking about.

Every now and then I went on a ride-out with a police officer. One day I was with this one officer and we got a call for a two car accident with injuries, and we were about two minutes away. This is the same officer I just talked about before he transferred to SWAT. We were responding with lights and siren and as we approached a traffic intersection we slowed down to make sure we didn't hit anyone as we went through the intersection.

As we approached everyone stopped except one taxicab driver kept going right through the intersection moving from our left as we hit the brakes. To my amazement, I swear the driver waived as he just kept on going. I yelled to the officer, "To heck with the accident go after that cab driver, he almost killed us!" We continued to the accident.

23. <u>Not On My Watch</u>! There is kind of an unwritten rule that no one dies while on airport property. It's an image or PR thing I guess, but it can't always be avoided. One day we had several calls coming in about a three car accident on the north end of the airport. We made our dispatch calls to the police units in the area. When EMS arrived on scene one of the drivers was a 72 year old female in critical condition (I think she had already passed) and they immediately determined they were going to transport her to the Parkland Hospital trauma unit in Dallas.

While enroute to Parkland the Paramedic in back called me on his cell phone telling me don't call out the crime scene guys yet. Now I learned why the unwritten rule. Anytime there is a death on airport property it has to be treated as a crime scene until it is proven that no alcohol, drugs or any other crime was involved. That would involve CID and a whole different set of rules and paperwork. A few minutes later the Paramedic called me back and informed me that they had arrived at Parkland hospital and the ER doctors had pronounced her dead and I could inform the police officers on scene.

24. **Not The Little Old Lady From Pasadena**. On another evening I was in dispatch taking calls when I received one from a lady passing by the west side of the airport on highway 360. She wanted to complain about some motorcycle drivers that were going very fast weaving in and out of traffic and seeing how far they could do "wheelies." She stated that "they had to be doing 100 mph, because when they came by me I was doing 80 mph."

I could just see this little old lady behind the wheel of her Buick, just barely tall enough to see over the steering wheel, with one hand on the wheel and a cell phone on the other. I responded by telling her to slow down, because I knew she was in a 60 mph speed zone and that I didn't want her to get hurt. I wanted to explained to her that most police will not get in a high speed chase with a motorcycle and that all I could do is call and notify the city they were going towards. I thought it best for her safety to hang up and pay attention to her driving so I told her I would take care of it and ended the call. Everyone in dispatch that evening got a good laugh out of that one when I played the voice recording back.

25. **Shots Fired**! I got medical calls, lost or stolen property calls, or missing person calls all the time, but this one call was a scary one. In this area the way cell phone signals bounce from one cell tower to another you get calls from people off airport in the surrounding highways and cities all the time. All you have to do is just determine which city to transfer the caller to. Well one day I got this call from some apartments that are located just off airport property in Irving. This was a problem area and there was no telling when or what type of call you might get from there. This is one I won't soon forget.

Me: "Airport 911, what's the location of your emergency?"

Caller: (Female) "I'm at the…. apartments and someone outside is shooting! Please help, what do I do!"

Me: "Ma'am stay in your apartment and don't go near the door or the windows. Do not hang up, stay on the line with me while I get the Irving police."

Irving: "Irving 911, what's the location of your emergency?"

Me: "This is the Airport 911 operator I have a caller on the line from the…. apartments reporting shots fired at her location."

Irving: Yes….(pause) that's us, our police are there on a drug raid."
I was tempted to yell, but I turned the lady over to Irving 911 and muted my phone and stayed on the line until she was told it was over. We were rather mad that Irving didn't give us a head's up on something so serious going down and located right off the end of a runway.

Another time we got a call from Grapevine 911 of a robbery and possible shooting at a private business just off airport property on the north side. The suspects were last seen running across State Highway 114, a major freeway in the area and onto airport property. We put out a call for all DFW patrol units to respond and the radios chatter went crazy.

We started getting phone calls from people on the north side that spotted them in and around parking lots and finally trying to hide in some tall grass that hadn't been cut. Of course we were getting all kinds of descriptions, 2 people, 3 people, 1 gun or no gun. When our SWAT officers arrived on scene that was it, they gave up without any trouble. Our

Chief was more than happy to turn them over to the Grapevine PD that was also on scene.

26. <u>Can You Hear The Laughter</u>? DPS 911 communications is located in the police station and in the control room there are several close circuit monitors for the cameras around the police station and two of them were in the jail focused on the holding cells. Late one night there was an intoxicated male, that had been processed in and he wanted to make a call. So he was given a cordless phone to make a call, but the jail officer stepped out.

About that time, I answered a 911 call and to my surprise it was him and as I observed him on one of the monitors he was saying he had been left alone, was being mistreated, he was hungry, and he needed to go to the bathroom. So, we're all getting a good laugh about him making a 911 call as I called the jail attendant who thought it was rather funny also.

Around 1:00 AM I got off shift and was driving home when my cell phone rang, and it was my son who was working the midnight shift at DPS Security. He asked me if I knew about the guy hanging himself in the jail just after I got off duty. It seems that not long after I left the guy hung himself (successfully) with his blanket. No one was laughing now; the jail attendant gave him a wool blanket instead of one that was design to rip if used like this. The jail attendant failed to follow several procedures that night.

Well, thank you very much, my time was over at dispatch. They had hired and trained several new folks, so I had to return to security. I had met some real fine people working there in dispatch and learned a lot that would help me later in security. It was fun while it lasted, but that job was just not my cup of tea for the long term.

27. <u>Your ID Is Fake.</u> One other assignment I got was a "Trusted Agent" in the Airport Access Control Office. This is where everyone who works at the airport from the CEO down has to apply for an airport identification badge. There are different badges each with varying levels of access codes programed into the badge micro-chip depending on your job location and requirements. In the performance of my job I would have access to the personal information and criminal history of individuals, thus the title and responsibility of "Trusted Agent."

When I first got there I was helping in the quality control room sorting applications that had been processed already. I couldn't do anything else until they got me set up with access to all of the computer programs so that I could process new applications. Once I was in the system I first learned how to do fingerprints on an automated scanning system which was the first step for a new application.

Once you obtained a good set of prints the computer would generate a report that was electronically sent to a third party company that did a background check. Within three to five days we would get a report back listing any conviction on your record from a traffic ticket to capital murder.

There was a police sergeant that worked in the office and it was his job to review each report and give the final clearance for a person to receive a badge or not based on their criminal history. Most of them came back on one page with no history found so he could go through them quickly. It was those that came back with several pages of history that took the Sargent some time.

Next I was trained to interview applicants, inter their personal information into the computer, take their picture and then produce a new badge with all of the proper access codes embedded on it for their job. All of this was done right there at my desk on the computer in a manner of eight to ten minutes.

Most days this is just a boring office job, but on occasion there would be something out of the ordinary happen. One day I was fingerprinting this guy for a job with a construction company. When I called him back I immediately noticed a tattooed tear drop under his right eye. Different tattoos can have a lot of different meanings, but I had heard that this one meant you had killed someone.

After I finished with him the very next person I did, same company, same tattoo! I took both applications back to the police sergeant, told him about the tattoos and that he might want to flag these guys reports when they came back. Sure enough several days later their reports came in and they both had prison records, but everything on them was over ten years ago, which was the statute of limitations we used. They both got their badges. I guess no matter what, everyone has to work somewhere.

You've seen shows on dumb criminals before, well we had our share also. Sometimes the FBI and police reports would come back and there would be outstanding arrest warrants on the individual. Well as soon as the sergeant would see this he would follow normal procedures to have this person called back in for their badge, except in this case they weren't going to get a badge. As soon as the person would check in he would be called back to the sergeant's office and placed under arrest, surprise!

When you applied for a badge you also had to provide two forms of identification, like a driver's license and a passport. I got to attend a training course on how to recognize fake or forged ID's that was presented by the airport U.S. Customs office. I really enjoyed that training and it was very useful in that job and also in security.

Because we had so many people working at the airport that were not American citizens you would see all kinds of different identifications and you wouldn't believe how many of them had been faked or altered. We would especially have problems with people from Mexico and several countries in South America. Some fakes were very good, but they just couldn't reproduce the security features in most of them.

Then you got some that made you want to laugh, like those that were made on a copy machine and then badly laminated. Some people would get a real passport but would try to tape a new identification page in it. I got pretty good at spotting the fakes and the altered ones. I was there because they were reorganizing and hiring new personnel. I enjoyed learning all that I did, but I needed to be out moving around and doing different things every day, not stuck in a cubicle.

28. **<u>TSA Reports An Active Shooter</u>**. About two weeks before my retirement I was on foot patrol on the secured side of Terminal B when I heard a radio call that made me stop in mid stride and a sudden fear swept over me. The dispatcher with a calm, but loud voice announced, "All units, active shooter Checkpoint Edward 30, all units respond." This was just after the five police officers were murdered in Dallas and three officers were gunned down in Baton Rouge, LA.

This is the one call I feared now and even when I still worked for TSA, because there is absolutely nothing to stop a person from walking right in from the curb and to start spraying bullets everywhere. Remember the TSA agent that was shot and killed at the LA airport in November 2013!

I immediately started for the nearest Terminal Link train platform which would have been the fastest way for me to get to Terminal E. As I heard all the police units reporting they were enroute, and as I reach the train platform, I heard the dispatcher come back on the radio with the announcement that it was a false alarm. FALSE ALARM how does something like that happen?

As it turns out some TSA agent had pushed the panic button at the checkpoint by mistake. Of course I was relieved, but mad at the same time that something like this happened and got so many of us alarmed. As radio calls continued you could hear the relief in everyone's voice, and it took several minutes for things to return to normal routine if there is such a thing as normal at an airport like DFW. We later found out that it was horseplay by two TSA agents that caused the alarm to be set off. I believe their service with TSA was no longer needed.

SECTION TWELVE
SOME FINAL THOUGHTS

Goodbye To A Friend

The following is a piece that I wrote back in 2015.

I learned on September 11, 2015, of the passing of a good friend and co-worker. Like me, he was in the military and around aviation most of his adult life. We often talked about our experiences during the Viet Nam War years and later his customer service position with Delta Airlines. After retiring from Delta, he came to work for TSA at the same time I was there. We worked on the same checkpoint teams at times and we both were volunteers at the airport USO Center for military service members and their families. Both of us had worked for DFW/DPS Airport Security for several years at the time of his passing. Everyone that knew him will remember that he was the type of person that no matter how he felt or what a situation might be, he always greeted you with a funny story or joke that lightened the mood.

A memorial service was held at a beautiful garden park with many of our co-workers, his family and close friends in attendance. Several testimonies and remembrances were given during the service, but it was one of the hospital chaplains that was with him in his final days that gave a testimony about his life that interested me.

He mentioned the "full measure" of one's life and this started me thinking. How should we measure one's life? Someone always mentions their family and how good a father, mother, brother and so on they were. We always talk about how successful in business or their job someone was. We look at their wealth and how much they gave to charity. Testimonies are given about their fame or what a good co-worker they were.

Then I started thinking how do I want my life measured? It won't be material wealth that's for sure. I had a very successful career in the Navy, and I have a beautiful family and grandkids I love very much, but that's not the sum total of who I am. There was only one answer I could understand, how does GOD measure a man? GOD's Word says:

1 Samuel 16:7 "GOD does not see man as man sees him. For man looks at the outward appearance, but the Lord looks at the heart." [60]

The heart speaks of a person's character and spirit. So often when we measure the worth of a person, we just look at the outward appearance, the success and failures of a person. GOD looks on the inside, the heart and the soul.

When the time comes will GOD see that I walked with integrity among family and friends? Will God see that I had a new heart through faith in Jesus Christ? Will others say he had a heart for the Lord and for the souls of everyone in his life? How will my life be measured? I hope God looks at my heart and sees His son Jesus Christ and the sacrifice He made for me on that cross at Calvary and not the sin of my life. Ask yourself the same question and look inward at your heart, what is the "full measure" of your life.

I don't know what the spiritual condition was of my friends heart and soul, but I pray he is in Heaven now swapping stories, telling jokes with all the Saints like he did with us and singing praises to our Lord. He'll be missed but always remembered. Rest in peace my friend.

Retirement

Retirement refers to the time of life when one chooses to permanently leave the workforce behind. What does that mean and what is really expected of a person in retirement? When I retired from the Navy I thought of retirement as just the end of my military service and now it was time for me to choose a civilian career. People have often asked me why I didn't go to work for the FAA since I was already an experienced air traffic controller. Well contrary to popular belief the government does participate in age discrimination in many job fields. By law at that time, you could not have reached your 31st birthday before your initial appointment with the FAA, I was 46 when I retired from the Navy and besides, being a controller at any busy facility is not for the faint at heart.

I was still too young to be really retired back then. But when I was fully vested with the DFW Airport Board I said goodbye. On my first full day of retirement I wasn't really sure of what I was supposed to feel or what I should plan to do next. It was a confusing time for me, I was so used to working every day for my pay, what is my purpose now. As I approached age 65, I applied for Medicare benefits, I was receiving my military pension and I would also start receiving Social Security payments along with my retirement pay from the airport.

I asked myself, when I got up each morning what will my schedule be? Will I have something to do or somewhere to go, other than another doctor's appointment or will I just sit in front of the TV as the hours and the days linger on? I would tell myself maybe I can find some volunteer work at a hospital or maybe at a VA assistance center.

As it turned out we have made several trips throughout the Midwest and overseas going to see our kids and grandkids and of course our antique hunting. I've got a knife collection now that is over 800 knives at present; I've started my own website gallery of knives; and I just published my first book for starting your knife collection. Titled "Folding Knives, Starting

Your Collection" and it's on sale now at Amazon.com. As you know I've written this book you've just read over a number of years and I have several others in the works. My newest hobby is repair and restoration of pocket knives and putting new handles on them from different materials.

So, as you can see, I didn't just sit around and wait for something to happen. I didn't just spend my days looking backwards and remembering. I've stayed busy and I enjoy each day of retirement. No matter what I do going forward the most important thing in my life is to see and enjoy my three children and thirteen grandchildren more than I did during my working years. To see them grow up to be fine Christian men and women. I hope I'm around many more years to tell our family story. I'm not too smart, but I hope I can pass on what little wisdom and knowledge I may still have. I hope with all my heart for peace in our nation, prosperity and a blessed life for my family and for all Americans. I hope.

Conclusion

You've heard some good things and a lot of negative things from me. I suppose most would label me as a negative personality, but that couldn't be further from the truth. I'm very positive that we will not lose the dreams of our founding fathers. That the documents that formed this nation and GOD's Holy Word will remain the guiding principles by which we are governed. I still have faith that GOD is in control and I believe that His promises and His plan will come to pass.

I hope I have not offended too many of you by my views, but like I said in the beginning I will not hide or deny my beliefs. As I conclude I would tell everyone, we won't agree on the many different issues, but that's ok because I know I'm right. All through the book I've told you why I'm politicly incorrect and why I'm right, but here it is one more time……GOD.

If you study God's word and pray for His leadership and understanding of any issue or situation you face, He will give you an answer. Remember God does not make mistakes, so if you're praying and following His word, you'll always be right and most likely politically incorrect.

Years ago, I was a fan of the TV show Star Trek, I guess it went along with my love of the U.S. space program. I remember that Commander Spock would always hold his hand up with a space between the ring finger and the middle finger and say, "Live long and prosper." With this parting let me say live your life daily for the honor and glory of God and may His bountiful blessings be with each of you daily.

David L. Roberts
Politically Incorrect

And Proud Of It

<u>References</u>

[1] Holy Bible (NKJV)

[2] Black Lives Matter website

[3] Brainy Quote website

[4] Better Help: The Psychology Behind Sense Of Entitlement, By Robert Porter February 05, 2021

[5] Merriam-Webster online dictionary

[6] Holy Bible NKJV

[7] Holy Bible NKJV

[8] Los Angeles Times By James Rainey July 23, 2012 12 AM PT

[9] Brainy Quotes website

[10] Merriam-Webster Dictionary Online

[11] https://www.wideopencountry.com/cowboy-hat-etiquette

[12] Brainy Quotes website

[13] Forbes Online by Michael T. Nietzel, Senior Contributor, Sep 9, 2020,07:14 am EDT

[14] National Education Association website

[15] OpenSecrets.org, Center for Responsive Politics

[16] Freedom Foundation, "NEA responds to fewer members by raising dues (again)" By Ben Straka July 7, 2020

[17] Merriam-Webster Online Dictionary

[18] EHS Today, Laura Walter, Sep 16, 2011

[19] Declaration of Independence

[20] Declaration of Independence

[21] Declaration of Independence

[22] Article V U.S. Constitution

[23] Colorado Fiscal Institute

[24] International Committee of the Red Cross

[25] Brainy Quotes

[26] United States Constitution

[27] The American Revolution against British Gun Control by David B. Kopel

[28] https://efsgv.org/reports/

[29] https://www.politifact.com/

[30] The Library of Congress.gov

[31] U.S. Declaration of Independence

[32] Dr. Martin Luther King, "I have a dream" speech August 28, 1963

[33] Anti-Defamation League, https://www.adl.org/racism

---

34 Tampa Bay Times, By Amy Sherman Published 6/23/2020, Updated 6/26/2020

35 Holy Bible (NKJV)

36 Holy Bible

37 Brainy Quotes

38 Billy Graham Evangelistic Association - billygraham.org

39 Cambridge online dictionary, https://dictionary.cambridge.org/

40 U.S. Constitution

41 Brainy Quotes

42 www.cityofdubuque.org/DocumentCenter

43 https://cdn.cnsnews.com/attachments/bias-language-guide-text-6-1.pdf

44 Brainy Quotes

45 www.fairus.org

46 www.migrationpolicy.org

47 www.statista.com

48 www.factcheck.org

49 Brainy Quotes

50 gabesfascinatingstories.blogspot.com

51 www.statista.com

52 Brainy Quotes

53 November 20, 2015 www.msnbc.com/mtp-daily

54 https://en.wikipedia.org/wiki/William_Thomas_Cummings

55 Brainy Quotes

56 Brainy Quotes

57 Holy Bible (NKJV)

58 www.mercurynews.com

59 www.afge.org

60 Holy Bible (NKJV)